Recognize and Respond to Emotional and Behavioral Issues in the Classroom

A Teacher's Guide

by

Andrew Jonathan Cole, Psy.D.

and

Aaron M. Shupp, Psy.D.

·P·A·U·L·H·
BROOKES
PUBLISHING CO®

Baltimore • London • Sydney

Paul H. Brookes Publishing Co.
Post Office Box 10624
Baltimore, Maryland 21285-0624
USA
www.brookespublishing.com

Typeset by Auburn Associates, Baltimore, Maryland.
Manufactured in the United States of America by
Versa Press Inc., East Peoria, Illinois.

The information provided in this book is in no way meant to substitute for a mental health practitioner's advice or expert opinion. Readers should consult a mental health professional if they are interested in more information. This book is sold without warranties of any kind, express or implied, and the publisher and authors disclaim any liability, loss, or damage caused by the contents of this book.

The individuals described in this book are fictional, based on composites or real people whose situations are masked and are based on the authors' actual experiences.

Library of Congress Cataloging-in-Publication Data

Cole, Andrew Jonathan.
  Recognize and respond to emotional and behavioral issues in the classroom :
  a teacher's guide by / Andrew Jonathan Cole and Aaron M. Shupp.
    p.   cm.
  Includes bibliographical references and index.
  ISBN 978-1-59857-223-0 (pbk. : alk. paper)
  ISBN 1-59857-223-7 (pbk. : alk. paper)
  1. Classroom management. 2. Behavior modification. 3. Problem children—
  Behavior modification. I. Shupp, Aaron M. II. Title.
  LB3013.C548 2012
  371.102'4—dc23   2012016058

British Library Cataloguing in Publication data are available from the British Library.

2016   2015   2014   2013   2012

10   9   8   7   6   5   4   3   2   1

Recognize and Respond to Emotional and Behavioral Issues in the Classroom

Contents

About the Authors

Andrew Jonathan Cole, Psy.D., is a licensed psychologist in New York and Maine. Currently, he conducts psychoeducational assessments and provides consultation for primary and secondary schools and mental health clinics. His diverse experience and training also include work in a university counseling center, private practice, outpatient and inpatient treatment facilities, and as the supervisor of a forensic rehabilitation program. As an individual and family psychotherapist, he supports struggling students with educational and behavioral problems and their caregivers.

Dr. Cole holds both a Psy.D. and M.A. in clinical psychology from Ferkauf Graduate School of Psychology, Yeshiva University; an M.A. in forensic psychology from John Jay College of Criminal Justice, City University of New York; and a B.A. in psychology from The Pennsylvania State University. He now lives and works in Maine, where he enjoys exploring the wilderness and writing essays and poetry in his spare time.

Aaron M. Shupp, Psy.D., is a licensed psychologist in New York. He has been providing psychological services to children, families, and adults for more than 10 years in settings that have included outpatient clinics, inpatient hospitals, and school-based treatment programs. His practice has included individual, family, and group psychotherapy; psychological assessments; systemic interventions; and consultation. Dr. Shupp has worked in both private practice and public service. His work also includes assessment and treatment of forensic patients, for which he has been called to provide expert testimony.

Dr. Shupp earned his bachelor's degree from Whittier College and graduated in 2004 from Pacific University School of Professional Psychology with his doctorate in clinical psychology.

Dr. Shupp previously worked as the only psychologist in a school-based treatment program for children with serious emotional and behavioral challenges. He worked closely with teachers, community providers, families, educational staff, and school administrators to develop and implement effective, individualized treatment plans for students ranging in age from 5 to 17.

FROM DRS. COLE AND SHUPP

We would like to thank our mutual friends and mentors, Dr. Kristina Berg and Dr. Brad Bennett, for their constant support, guidance, and inspiration. Their compassion and understanding have seen us through personal and professional challenges, and we consider them models of professionalism and magnanimity.

We also thank the clinicians and staff at the Clinton Therapy and Testing Center for their excellent work, kindness, and friendship.

To my wife and children—for all you teach me,
and for leaving me in awe of life's possibilities

—Aaron M. Shupp

in research literature. They are also the strategies we have found helpful in our clinical and consulting experiences.

The recommendations contained in this book are in no way intended as a replacement for structured intervention programs. Formalized intervention programs play an important role in behavior management. Educators who have training in such models are likely to find them useful and effective. These programs, however, often require formal assessment of student needs, additional training for educators, and collaboration with other professionals who are trained to oversee the implementation of these approaches. This guidebook is designed to be a starting point for everyday challenges.

Although the recommendations are based on well-established psychological principles, they are not unique to any specific research findings. Our approach to creating this guidebook was to compile recommendations we might give if asked to provide consultative input on the spot; the recommendations are therefore informed by, but not directly connected to, any specific research. This style of organization permitted a more fluid, accessible, and readable guidebook for daily use.

WHEN TO USE

We envision certain situations in which this guidebook will be most useful. The most obvious scenario for using this guidebook may be when your standard behavior management techniques are not working for a specific situation. However, it will also be helpful to review the recommendations when you are simply questioning whether your approach is likely to be effective. Sometimes, just finding that you are on the right track can be comforting and reassuring and may help you to stay the course through a challenging time. Of course, when you find yourself faced with a novel or unfamiliar situation, it may be helpful to seek out recommendations and see how they match up with the approach you might have instinctively taken.

FORMAT

To allow quick and efficient access to pertinent information, each chapter follows a consistent format. The title of each chapter reflects a common problem that might be observed in the classroom. Diagnostic terms and labels are avoided because the reader is not expected to be in the role of formally assessing or diagnosing the student. A case study is presented first for the purpose of illustrating the challenges that might be present. Specific, observable behaviors are then noted in the section "What You

Might See." "Description of Problems" is where you will find general information on the problem being addressed, such as possible causes, associated problems, and how the problem is being defined for the purpose of the chapter. The Recommendations section is divided into three segments: "Classroom Structure," "Collaborating with the Student," and "Collaborating with the Family/Caregivers." The section titled "Referral to an Administrator, Counselor, or Mental Health Professional" provides guidelines for when additional consultation or referral may be necessary. Finally, "What to Expect" illustrates how the recommendations might be applied to the case study.

After each chapter, you will find additional resources either in the form of a worksheet you can reproduce and use as needed, an exercise to clarify where to start for your specific situation, or an informational handout. In addition, discussion questions are presented at the end of each chapter to spark your own further exploration of the topic or to be used in peer reading or study groups.

TIPS FOR USING THIS BOOK

The first chapter of this guidebook reviews some general principles of classroom management and behavioral interventions. We encourage you to become familiar with these concepts because they are the foundation of many of the recommendations that follow. With an understanding of the underlying principles, you will be well equipped to creatively adapt the recommendations to your particular situation. And remember, any strategy you implement will need to be consistently carried out to be effective. Unfortunately, this often means enduring periods of time that bring to mind the old adage, "Sometimes things get worse before they get better." Change does not happen quickly, but it does happen!

Collaboration is stressed as a key element of successful interventions throughout this guidebook. Perhaps the most important form of collaboration, however, will be the collaboration between you and the recommendations that follow. Whether you are a seasoned teacher or preparing for your first student teaching experience, you bring a wealth of personal knowledge and experience. From your first day as a teacher, you begin acquiring knowledge about what has worked and what has not worked with similar students, when you have felt successful and when you have felt ineffective, and, most important, the individual nature of each student. In fact, other than family members, it is often a teacher who knows a child best. The recommendations in this guidebook will make the greatest impact when you put them in the context of your expertise and knowledge and tailor them to your specific situation.

LIMITATIONS

The recommendations contained in this guidebook should not be considered psychotherapy and, as previously stated, are not part of a structured intervention program. These strategies are designed to be implemented without any additional training, and are flexible enough to tailor to your particular situation. When addressing specific problem behaviors, however, caution should be taken to work within your area of competence and training. Avoid assuming the role of counselor or diagnostician. As a person who is dedicated to helping young people, you may certainly be willing to help a child through an emotional or behavioral challenge, and may even feel it is your responsibility to do so. Similarly, it can be tempting to conclude that a student has a particular disorder or condition, but doing so puts you at risk of causing harm to the student, alienating the family, and being held personally liable. Maintain awareness of the limits of your training and expertise, and be mindful of the situations and circumstances in which you may feel compelled to reach beyond your qualifications. Many competent, well-intentioned professionals cause problems for themselves and the individuals they are trying to help when they lose sight of their role and find themselves working outside their area of expertise.

This guidebook should not be a substitute for consultation with colleagues and supervisors or for referral to other professionals. Each chapter will conclude with guidelines for when to consult an administrator, counselor, or mental health professional. There are, of course, some instances in which referral or consultation is always warranted. Anytime you suspect abuse or mistreatment, it will be beneficial to initiate a referral or consultation, and it is your legal mandate to follow all state and local reporting guidelines. Similarly, your district or state may require a specific course of action in cases of suspected, reported, or observed bullying, whether in your classroom, outside of the classroom, or online. Direct suicidal statements; statements or behavior that reflect hopelessness, despair, or worthlessness; any other reason for suspecting that a student may harm him- or herself or others; and reported or observed self-injury or neglect of basic self-care should always be taken seriously and reported immediately. Because this topic cannot be adequately covered in this guidebook, we strongly encourage all teachers to seek out training in how to identify signs associated with risk of suicide, abuse, and violence. Although not as clearly identifiable, any abrupt changes in a student's mood, behavior, or academic or social functioning should also warrant prompt referral or consultation. In short, this book is not intended to replace legal, ethical, or professional requirements for acting to ensure the safety of all students.

Chapter 1

Guiding Concepts

There are many high-quality resources on classroom management. This chapter contains information on some of the foundational concepts that underlie many of the recommendations in the following chapters. However, the reader who is interested in more comprehensive resources on classroom management is referred to the Resources and Recommendations for Further Reading list at the end of the book.

Few concepts in psychology are so widely accepted that they have become ubiquitous in the literature. We will present three such concepts here. These principles form the foundation of many psychological interventions and treatment programs. They can be thought of as necessary ingredients of a successful intervention, but not the complete recipe!

Whether working with a student or guardian, your effectiveness will be greatly influenced by three factors: establishing a positive relationship, setting realistic and attainable goals, and using effective reinforcement. Pertinent information and recommendations related to each of these areas are presented below.

POSITIVE RELATIONSHIPS

- Focus on establishing a relationship built on respect, validation, and collaboration. Students and caregivers alike will be more open to working with you when they feel as if their perspectives are understood and valued and when their input is solicited.
- Find at least one quality you really like about each student. When this seems most difficult, it is most important!

- Find small ways to show each student that he or she is important to you, such as greeting the student in the morning, remembering something specific that the student shared, and asking questions. Even if you do not get an obvious reaction, never underestimate the impact of simple questions or statements, such as, "John, you said you were going to go camping this weekend; how did it go?" or, "I know you're really good at building things, Tara, so I may need your help setting up for a special activity later."

- With students, make an effort to find out about their interests. Notice what they say about themselves and their values through dress and personal accessories. Most students will quickly reject anything that looks like faking knowledge or interest in a topic. Rely instead on the natural desire most students have to share their interests with others. Look for opportunities to allow the student to teach you something.

- With parents, acknowledge their expertise and experience, and make clear your affection for the student and desire for the student to do well in your class. If parents or guardians think that you do not like the student or that you are more interested in punishing the student than in helping him or her, you will quickly lose their support. With particularly frustrating behavior, this may mean taking time to write down the student's positive qualities and your goal for the student in your classroom, so that these are clear in your mind and you can communicate them clearly to the guardians.

- Maintain professional boundaries. It may seem easier and faster to form a relationship as a friend or confidant, but putting in the time and effort to develop a strong relationship within firm professional boundaries will foster feelings of security, comfort, and trust among your students and will teach them about healthy relationships.

- Avoid using labels such as *attention-deficit/hyperactivity disorder (ADHD)* or *autism spectrum* with students or guardians unless they have volunteered this information or they are comfortable using such language as contained in the school's psychoeducational assessment of the child. Focus instead on direct observations and your willingness to help in connecting them with whatever resources may be helpful, such as a school counselor.

- Try not to take negative behavior personally. Remind yourself that the difficulties the student is displaying are the result of many complex factors and that your willingness to help is not the same as assuming responsibility to fix the problem. Lasting change usually involves the efforts of many people and requires the full commitment of the student and guardians.

SETTING GOALS

- Know what your ultimate goal is for a student, but identify the small steps needed to get to that goal. Understand where the student is now so that you can begin identifying all the small steps that will be needed to reach the larger goal. It is often helpful to write down on one side of a paper what you observe of the student now and, on the other side of the paper, what you would hope to see from this student. As the student progresses, write down the steps still needed to move closer to the desired goal.

- Each small step should be attainable. Setting goals that are too far from the student's starting point can lead to frustration and discouragement for both you and the student. Setting attainable goals leads to feelings of success, confidence, and optimism. Each small goal that is met will create positive momentum toward the next one. Steps can be as small as a student going from raising his or her hand once a week to twice a week, or increasing the amount of time spent focused on an assignment from 3 minutes at a time to 5 minutes at a time.

- Remember that working toward small goals is not letting the student off the hook or lowering expectations. You know what you are working toward with the student, and you are actually using a more effortful and time-consuming approach, but such an approach is much more likely to be effective. When you feel discouraged, it sometimes helps to reflect on a difficult goal that you set for yourself and achieved. This achievement likely involved a series of small milestones (think of your own educational experience!).

- Goals should be clear and observable. It should be easy to determine whether the goal has been met because it can be observed.

- Goals should be explicit. Let the student know what he or she is working toward, and, when appropriate, seek the student's input in developing goals. The more the student feels like a participant in the process, the more motivated he or she will be and the more each success will be internalized or seen as the result of his or her own efforts.

REINFORCEMENT

- *Reinforcement* simply means causing a behavior to become more frequent. It can be done by providing something desirable (positive reinforcement or positive reward) or taking away something undesirable (negative reinforcement or negative reward). Reinforcements are effective in bringing about lasting change. Punishment refers to

Chapter 2

Poor Concentration and Impulsive Behavior

Dana is a student in your second-grade class. She is creative, outgoing, and full of energy. As the school year begins, you notice that she seems to have difficulty waiting her turn in group activities, speaks without waiting to be called on, and is often engaged in off-task behavior. Frequently, in-class redirection has no effect, so you decide to speak with her privately after school. During your conversation, Dana seems remorseful and sincere in her desire to improve her classroom behavior. You can tell she has good intentions, so you decide she is merely having difficulty adjusting to her new grade level. The behavior continues, however, and you find yourself increasingly frustrated by what appears to be her lack of effort.

As the school year progresses, you notice that other students appear to be bothered when Dana does not wait her turn or blurts out answers. They sometimes complain when she fidgets in her seat and acts intrusively. They do not particularly want to be on her team for group activities. She does not seem to go with the flow in unstructured activities, such as recess. She is seen as bossy, loud, and rude. Although she is outgoing and tries to make friends, she cannot maintain friendships very well. Dana attempts to use humor to connect with other students. As she tries to establish a role as the class clown, Dana, with increasing frequency, makes loud, disruptive, and off-topic statements. Consequently, you have to address her behavior with progressively more severe discipline measures, including administrative referrals. Because she is regularly in trouble, her futile attempts to fit in with her classmates have led to further isolation and rejection.

WHAT YOU MIGHT SEE

- Has difficulty following along with classroom activities, directions, or lessons
- Frequently appears to be fidgeting in her seat, looking around the room, responding to minor distractions, playing with pencils or papers, or attempting to get the attention of peers
- Calls out answers or irrelevant statements at inappropriate times
- Interrupts the teacher or peers when they are talking
- Jumps out of her seat to perform tasks unrelated to the lesson
- Routinely forgets homework or turns in assignments that are messy or incomplete
- Has difficulty making and keeping friends or otherwise demonstrates poor social skills
- May appear to have a short temper or an inability to follow directives

DESCRIPTION OF PROBLEMS

Poor concentration and impulsive behavior can be related to biological factors or to skill deficits related to maintaining appropriate behaviors in school settings. Other factors, such as nutrition, anxiety, or low mood, can also lead to (or exacerbate) these problems. Students with learning disabilities sometimes appear to act out or lose interest in lessons when they are confronted with topics or tasks that are particularly difficult for them. Before these learning disabilities have been diagnosed, such students may simply appear to have behavior problems.

Children with poor concentration and impulsivity frequently have co-occurring struggles with academic performance and socialization. Sometimes, caregivers are aware of their child's lack of concentration in school because these difficulties are exhibited in many areas of the child's life. Other times, the child does not display these behaviors outside of the classroom because she is able to function more effectively in less structured settings. Many of these students are unable to recall expectations for their behavior in different settings, and they may require reminders about how to act in school, sports, social situations, or meetings with adults.

Some of these children have been diagnosed with attention-deficit/hyperactivity disorder (ADHD) by health care professionals. However, students who exhibit a lack of concentration and impulsivity do not necessarily have a mental health disorder, and, even if they do, they could be experiencing something other than ADHD. Further, students with these problems could be at risk for peer rejection, withdrawal from academic challenges, and low self-esteem. They can also become vulnerable to more serious problems, such as substance abuse and involvement in the legal system.

Recommendations

~~~~~~~~~~~~~~~ CLASSROOM STRUCTURE ~~~~~~~~~~~~~~~

Ask Yourself

Does the student have difficulty paying attention and sitting still or difficulty organizing and completing assignments?

Your answer will help you focus your interventions.

- *Use positive reinforcement:* Make use of frequent praise, encouragement, or rewards for positive behaviors, even with the most challenging students. Such feedback will likely lead to increased motivation and improved understanding of specific expectations.

- *Individualize rewards:* Make the rewards meaningful and important to the student. Rewards work only if the child is motivated by them.

- *Apply consequences consistently:* When referring the student for disciplinary action or otherwise giving consequences for negative behaviors, ensure that the student reliably receives similar consequences for similar misbehaviors.

- *Do not take it personally:* Although disruptive behaviors can be extremely frustrating for educators, they are often an expression of problems or innate tendencies that reach far beyond the classroom.

- *Seat front and center:* Seating the student in the front and center of class may reduce distractions while helping the child focus on the teacher. Sometimes sitting to the side or near the teacher's desk also proves beneficial.

- *Use organizers:* Encourage the use of calendars, checklists, filing folders, flashcards, sticky notes, wristwatch alarms, or anything else that improves organizational skills.

- *Review assignments:* Suggest that the student routinely review class assignments at a regular time each day, preferably before the end of the school day. This allows time to ask another student or teacher for misplaced, or already forgotten, assignments.

- *Encourage mental breaks:* Suggest that an easily distracted student take a 2- to 3-minute mental break every 10–20 minutes to rest her mind and to regain focus. It is best to take these mental breaks before the student becomes fatigued.

- *Keep a record:* Have the student record in a notebook the time and subject she is working on when she starts to lose her attention during class. This serves to increase awareness of when extra effort, reminders, or other organizational interventions are most useful, and it teaches the student to pay closer attention to her own habits.

- *Simplify tasks:* Help the student reduce complex tasks into smaller, easier-to-follow steps.

- *Try to be patient:* Recognize that it may take months or years for some students to improve on these problems.

Keep in Mind

- Changes may be small at first, but persistence will pay off.

- Review, organize, and record.

- Individualize approaches, stay consistent, and break it down.

COLLABORATING WITH STUDENTS

Ask Yourself

In what situations has the student appeared to feel successful?

When has the student appeared to focus her attention?

You can build on even small signs that the student is able to focus and achieve goals.

- *Work together:* Ask the child what will help her focus in class. Often, the student is not a participant in the creation of her own educational or behavioral interventions. However, the most successful approaches involve strong collaboration among school staff, the student, and the student's family.

- *Encourage personal responsibility:* Treat children with attention and concentration problems with compassion and understanding for their struggles, but do not allow labels such as ADHD to become justifications for problematic behaviors. Many children have tendencies or limitations that lead to maladaptive behaviors. However, such students often do best if they learn to take responsibility for as much of their behavior as is reasonable.

- *Keep challenges in perspective:* Remind the student that attention problems, distractibility, impulsivity, or diagnoses such as ADHD do not mean that she is unintelligent or lacking in potential. Quite to the contrary, many children with these problems blossom with added structure and encouragement to achieve their fullest potential.

- *Use repetition:* Repeat instructions or ask the child to repeat them if she has difficulty recalling assignments.

- *Set realistic goals:* Using smaller, specific goals that are achievable in the near term is important for increasing the child's sense of accomplishment and, consequently, her motivation.
- *Win the student's attention:* Ensure that the student is facing you and making eye contact before speaking to her. This will greatly improve the student's ability to attend to what you say.
- *Be creative!* As you know, every student is a little different and will respond to slightly different approaches.

Keep in Mind

- Make the student a partner in creating change.
- Small successes sustain the student's motivation.

COLLABORATING WITH THE FAMILY/CAREGIVERS

Ask Yourself

What have the caregivers said they tried and found helpful or not helpful?

What has been successful in the classroom that can be continued at home?

Providing caregivers with a few specific suggestions about study habits can make a big difference in the child's performance.

- *Practice skills at home:* Tell the caregivers what organizational systems are being used in school, and encourage their use at home. Remind parents that good organizational skills at home lead to effective skills in school.
- *Gather information:* Encourage family to read relevant books and resources on improving attention and decreasing impulsivity.
- *Set expectations:* Ask the parent to remind the child about the expectations for school before leaving home and to set a small goal for the student for that day (if this is done, put in communication journal so the teacher will know).
- *Praise the student's progress:* Encourage parents or caregivers to commend or reward specific behaviors from the previous day or that morning.
- *Use effective study habits:* Homework should be done in a quiet area without distractions. Set a time period in which to work. Take small, clearly defined breaks (5–10 minutes), and then resume work for a clearly defined time. Reward the child after the work period is complete, and not before (e.g., let the child play a game or talk on the phone for 30 minutes).
- *Use written messages:* Have daily or weekly communication between the school and home (e.g., through a communication journal) to convey how the student did, any problems that day or week, and when the problems occurred. Assignments can also be conveyed to caregivers in this manner.
- *Schedule conferences:* Parents should feel free to request regular conferences with the teacher to coordinate the techniques and rewards that are most

effective in school and at home. The child's strengths, interests, and progress should also be addressed.

- *Encourage constructive pastimes:* Emphasize leisure activities that tap into the child's areas of strength (e.g., art, music, athletics). The student should avoid passive activities, such as video games. Parents are sometimes encouraged to see their child focus on a video game for an extended period of time. However, many video games are not helpful in teaching children to sustain attention because the stimulation is intense and frequently changes.

- *Choose structured social activities:* Parents should promote activities that are well supervised and planned (e.g., Boy Scouts/Girl Scouts, organized sports, after-school programs). Such activities are more likely to be successful experiences for the child.

Keep in Mind

- Study skills practiced at home will contribute to success in the classroom.

- Encourage caregivers to provide outlets for the child's energy and creativity at home while also developing new work skills.

REFERRAL TO AN ADMINISTRATOR, COUNSELOR, OR MENTAL HEALTH PROFESSIONAL

Consider referral to an administrator, counselor, or health professional when

- You have exhausted all the methods for which you have the time or resources, but the student continues to struggle to follow rules, attend to lessons, or complete assignments.

- There is a notable increase in the student's problems and/or a noticeable decline in her academic performance.

- The problems are causing significant distress for the student or peers.

- The student is persistently disrupting your ability to teach.

- Parents express concerns as well as uncertainty about how to manage the child's behaviors.

Keep in Mind

- There are many health care professionals who help children and families cope with these attention and impulsivity problems.

- Occasionally, the student's difficulties in class are indicative of a larger or more pervasive problem.

- Consulting with a colleague or other professional at your school may not only lead to benefits for the child but also may help reduce your own stress.

WHAT TO EXPECT

Although Dana is having difficulty in several areas, you decide to first target her difficulty with blurting out answers, questions, or unrelated comments because this habit is highly disruptive to the classroom. On individually meeting with her, you find out that she loves music and enjoys talking about her favorite singers. You find common ground in that she wants to do well in your class and does not want any more office referrals. She mentions that her parents take away television and computer time when she gets an office referral. You make it clear to Dana that you are committed to helping her and that you believe in her. You suggest that she sit up front so that she will not be distracted by the other students. Dana is not eager to move to the front, but, with encouragement, she agrees to give it a try. You also suggest that Dana work on not interrupting the class and that, when she wants to say something, she should try raising her hand and waiting to be called on. By proposing this goal, you have introduced organization and priorities in what likely seems to Dana a set of overwhelming problems. You know that when she is successful with this goal, her self-confidence will grow and that other problems can be targeted later.

When you call Dana's parents, you find they are clearly concerned with her struggles and have been trying on their own to address them with Dana. They tell you that she loves listening to music at home and takes great pride in being able to help them with household activities. They also tell you that she recently got a set of books that she enjoys because the stories revolve around a young musician. Her parents seem eager to help, and they are appreciative that you reached out to them. You share with them the goal that you set with Dana and suggest starting a communication notebook that can go between school and home. You also suggest that, in the notebook, you will put a copy of the daily schedule. Although her parents suggest putting in a checkmark for a good day and a minus sign for a bad day, you recommend putting in the daily class schedule and tracking how many times Dana raises her hand during each activity and how many times she blurts something out during each activity. You explain that, by starting this way, you can help Dana see when she is raising her hand more, and thus she can see improvement. Because Dana's parents seem eager to help, you suggest that she can bring one of her new books to school; when she raises her hand more than she blurts out during a particular activity, she can get 3–5 minutes to read her book in the reading corner during the transition time. In addition, her parents work with you on an after-school reward program, in which she can stay after school to help you with a special project and listen to the radio if she has two or fewer instances of disruptive behavior for the entire day. You share with them your belief that Dana can achieve these goals and continue to progress toward other improvements.

DISCUSSION QUESTIONS

1. Looking back on your experience as a student, were there any times you had a hard time paying attention or staying focused? How did you get through these challenges? Was there anything about those situations that seemed to contribute to these difficulties?

2. In the classes that you currently teach, are there any activities in which it is harder to keep the attention of your students? When do you find it easiest to keep the attention of most of your students?

3. What have you tried in the past to help students who were struggling with concentration problems or impulsiveness? Looking back, were these interventions successful? Is there anything you would have done differently?

4. What are likely to be some of the worries, concerns, or fears of parents who have a child struggling with concentration problems or impulsivity?

5. If you determine that a student needs additional help, whom would you contact first? What are the resources in your community?

Note to Educators: The following form is an example of a simple reminder sheet that can be used to help students stay organized and on task each day. You can modify this format to fit the needs of each individual. Or, you can develop a standard organization sheet for any student who might benefit from it. This example is for use at the end of each day. It is designed for a secondary school student. However, a similar checklist can be developed for primary school students or formatted to be reviewed after each class or at the end of each week. Parents can also be encouraged to create a checklist for each evening to ensure that all homework is completed.

Daily Assignment Checklist

Check the boxes for the tasks you have completed today. You should review this sheet at least 30 minutes before you leave school for the day. If any of these tasks are not yet complete, you should complete them before leaving school.

☐ Turn in all assignments that were due today. (Check your calendar and daily assignment checklists to see what was due today.)

☐ Check to make sure that new assignment sheets are placed in the right folders. For example, science sheets should be in the folder labeled *Science*.

☐ Check to make sure that you have all of the books needed for tonight's homework.

Book _____

Assignment _____ Due _____

Book _____

Assignment _____ Due _____

Book _____

Assignment _____ Due _____

Book _____

Assignment _____ Due _____

No book needed   Assignment _____ Due _____

_____   _____

☐ If you are not sure whether you have homework in a particular class, ask a classmate or a teacher before you leave today.

☐ Long-term projects that were assigned today

Project: _____

Class: _____ Due: _____

Project: _____

Class: _____ Due: _____

☐ Make a note on your school calendar for **all** new assignments.

☐ Write down reminders for anything else you need to do tonight or this week:

_____

_____

_____

Chapter 3

Low Moods

Justin is a student in your 10th-grade math class. He has been in your class for several months and has maintained average grades. Although you pride yourself on forming a connection with each of your students, Justin has seemed harder to reach. He is generally polite, and he even laughs sometimes with other students, but for the most part he seems somewhat distant and not very engaged with you or his peers.

In the past several weeks, Justin's grades have been dropping. He appears to have a hard time concentrating and seems to not retain the information you are teaching. He sometimes looks tired in class. It seems like he is not putting forth enough effort, but you do not want to give up on him. When you attempt to discuss your concerns with him, he appears irritated by your efforts and seems to withdraw more. On one occasion, you notice that while the other students are working on class material, he is drawing on a piece of paper. When you walk by to see how you can help, he covers his paper and puts his head down.

In your conversations with other teachers, you hear of similar problems in other classes. One of your colleagues describes him as "on edge." Another is concerned that Justin had to be counseled on what he needed to do to improve his grade; he was in danger of failing and did not seem to care. Some of your colleagues express worry about him; others seem frustrated by his lack of motivation and are becoming increasingly convinced that attempts to reach him are falling short because he just is not interested in school. You find yourself wondering whether he is simply a loner or whether something is bothering him that he is not talking about. It seems like a struggle to find a way to reach him. You want to provide him with support, but you find yourself feeling discouraged and questioning your approach.

WHAT YOU MIGHT SEE

- Seems withdrawn, disinterested, or lacking in motivation
- Difficulty concentrating
- Irritable or easily frustrated
- Increased displays of anger
- Appears tired, distant, or disheveled
- Difficulty identifying future goals or plans
- Difficult to find his interests
- May not smile or laugh often, or easily becomes tearful
- Shows little emotional reaction, whether positive or negative
- May have apparent scratches, cuts, or burns on body
- Sudden changes in clothing style or appearance, such as wearing long sleeves almost exclusively (to cover self-injury) or wearing predominantly dark clothing
- Focus on dark or morbid themes in conversation, art, or writing
- May make statements suggesting thoughts of harming or killing self
- Feelings of concern among teachers: fear for the student's safety, frustration or rejection when attempts to engage him are not successful, or discouragement at the student's lack of motivation
- Perceptions among some adults or peers that the student is lethargic, overly sensitive, or "doing it for attention"

DESCRIPTION OF PROBLEMS

Low moods can be the result of situational stress, such as the loss of a loved one, social problems, family discord, or major life changes. Internal distress, such as disappointment caused by failing to meet unreasonably high expectations for oneself, can also affect mood. Biological factors, such as the lack of healthful diet or exercise, medical problems, or a genetic predisposition to mood problems may also play a role. In addition, other factors, such as exposure to traumatic events or use of substances, can contribute to low moods. The reason for the low mood can, and often does, involve several factors. Therefore, caution has to be taken not to rush to conclusions about the cause or to assume that the student will know what precipitated the negative feelings.

Students who experience a low mood may demonstrate very recognizable signs, such as easily becoming tearful, appearing lethargic, and withdrawing from social interactions. Sometimes, however, children and adolescents with low moods demonstrate increased irritability or agitation. In addition, the child may be experiencing other thoughts or feelings that are not directly observable, such as feelings of hopelessness or worthlessness. Self-injury, such as scratching or cutting arms or other body parts, may be associated with low moods. However, this behavior can also be the result of other problems. Students with low moods are at increased risk for suicide (see "When to Refer" section later in this chapter). Negative emotional states may also contribute to problems with substance abuse, social isolation, school avoidance, careless or reckless behavior, and poor academic achievement.

Sometimes, low moods are considered synonymous with depression. The term *depression,* however, is often used to refer to a larger set of symptoms that are captured in diagnostic labels such as *Major Depressive Disorder.* Using the term *depression,* therefore, may lead to misunderstandings about the nature and severity of the problem. Individuals who experience low moods do not necessarily have mental health disorders. Some problems with low moods can be relatively short term, cause limited disruption to the individual's life, and improve without any significant intervention. However, a student experiencing a short-term disruption in mood is still likely to benefit from extra support in the classroom.

Recommendations

 CLASSROOM STRUCTURE

Ask Yourself

What specific problems is the student having in my class (e.g., withdrawing from group exercises, not completing assignments, limiting involvement in class activities)?

- *Maintain realistic expectations:* Keep in mind that your role is to provide a supportive learning environment. Do not put pressure on yourself to "solve" the student's problems.

- *Do not single out:* If a student's academic problems seem related to the recent onset of a low mood, placing that student at the front-center of the room to help him pay attention may cause the student to feel there is a spotlight on his problems. When possible, collaborate with the student to find seating arrangements, workgroups, or activities in which he is comfortable and interested.

difficulty he is experiencing. The student may feel overwhelmed and not be able to prioritize concerns, and he may not be able to take an optimistic view of the situation improving. If this appears to be the case, guide the student by suggesting goals and expectations, and allow the student to follow your lead.

- *Goal setting:* For students with low moods, you may have to set small, attainable, short-term goals. For example, it may be helpful to provide a student with a specific task to complete for a particular class period, rather than provide instructions for a multistep project that involves work over several days.

- *Benchmarks:* For assignments that involve work outside of the classroom, students may benefit from being given smaller benchmarks and having time to check in with you about their progress at regular intervals. For example, on a project given over several weeks, break the task into smaller steps, and schedule regular meetings to check in on progress for each of the steps (every week, for example). Provide encouragement or positive feedback at each benchmark.

- *Use reflective listening:*
  - Acknowledge that you have heard the student by reflecting back part of what was said.
  - Provide empathy by focusing on the feeling behind what is being said (e.g., "I can see you're feeling really down right now," or, "It seems like that problem is really troubling you").
  - If you are speaking with a younger child, consider kneeling down or sitting to put yourself on the child's eye level. This can help the child feel more comfortable sharing with an adult.
  - Avoid giving a lot of advice all at once or trying to solve the problem too quickly.

- *Responding to disclosures:* If the student does share that there is a problem in his life that is affecting him in school, you do not necessarily need to elicit detailed information. Remember, that is why your school counselors, administrators, or mental health professionals are there! Remind the student that you care about how he feels and that you want him to have the appropriate support. Then, connect the student with the professional who can help him cope with these difficulties.

- *Connecting with resources:* Do not be afraid to acknowledge the limitations of what you can do (e.g., "This seems really important to me, and I'm glad you told me how you are feeling. I may not be the best person to help with these kinds of problems, but I would like to help you get in touch with someone who is. Can I set up an appointment for you to go see the school counselor? I'd be happy to go with you to introduce you, if you'd like").

Keep in Mind

- Helping a student with a low mood takes an entire team! Focus your efforts on helping the student succeed in your class, and rely on other professionals when needed.

- Do not gauge your success by whether or not the child's mood improves. This may take time and effort from other supports in the student's life. If you are doing your best to support the student in your class and you make a referral when needed, then you are succeeding.

∼∼∼ COLLABORATING WITH THE FAMILY/CAREGIVERS ∼∼∼

Ask Yourself

What are the most important observations to share with the caregivers? What specific behaviors or statements suggest that the child is experiencing low moods?

What will I say to the family if they are indifferent to my concerns or if they share very personal family problems with me?

[Hint: Keep the focus on how the student's apparent low moods affect his schoolwork.]

- *Set and maintain boundaries:* Your role is to share your concerns and to offer your support as an educator. However, families may sometimes pull for you to become overly involved in their personal problems. When interacting with the caregivers, be very clear on your role and the limits of what you can and cannot do. Your role as a problem solver relates to your particular class and, perhaps, to the student's general educational needs. Becoming highly involved in a child's or a family's personal problems may not serve you or the student well.

- *Share objective observations:* When providing feedback to caregivers, emphasize what you have directly observed (e.g., the student is tired in class, not as concerned with his grades as before, saying he feels sad, expressing negative attitudes, isolating himself or herself, acting indifferent to encouragement). Be careful not to label a child as having depression; this is best left to your school's or the family's mental health professionals. However, you may be one of the most observant and attuned adults in a child's life. So, your objective observations are extremely valuable.

- *Expect the unexpected:* Be prepared for families that react in surprising ways. Some families will be highly responsive and appreciative for your feedback about their child's attitude or mood in class. Certain families may act uninterested or even angry, viewing your objective observations as an intrusion into their personal lives. And some families will disclose more personal information about what is going on in their lives than you ever wanted to know.

- *Visualize your response:* Consider visualizing how you would handle each of these family responses before you pick up the phone or start the meeting. Two minutes of visualizing how you will handle a challenging response can do a lot to prepare you. For example, if a caregiver does not seem to value your observations about the child's change in attitude or social withdrawal, be prepared to explain how these changes are affecting the student's performance in school, making it an important issue for his education.

- *Use your resources:* If you and another school professional (e.g., counselor or psychologist) share the same concerns, consider meeting with the caregivers together. You may both have useful observations from different perspectives, and your collaboration conveys your professionalism and teamwork to the family.

Keep in Mind

- You do not need to be pulled into a role as family therapist. The family and other professionals should work to solve any personal problems outside of the classroom.

- It is better to avoid stigmatizing labels, such as, "He is suffering from depression." Leave the diagnoses to health care professionals. Sometimes, families react to diagnostic labels with defensiveness or shame. Health care professionals are trained to explain these diagnoses in a way that lessens such reactions.

REFERRAL TO AN ADMINISTRATOR, COUNSELOR, OR MENTAL HEALTH PROFESSIONAL

Ask Yourself

Do I have any concern for this student's safety? Has the student made reference to death, not being here anymore, or feeling hopeless or worthless?

Have I noticed any unusual or patterned abrasions on the student's body?

Do the signs of a low mood significantly affect his schoolwork or ability to engage in classroom activities with other students?

Consider such a step when

- A student makes direct statements about suicide or general comments about death; "not being here"; feeling hopeless, helpless, or worthless; or wanting to get away from everything. Other possible indicators that a student may be considering suicide include giving away possessions, saying goodbye to friends and acquaintances, drawing pictures or writing stories depicting himself or herself as dead or dying, or a quick shift from a low mood to a relieved, positive mood. If you have any concern about a student harming himself or herself, refer immediately to school mental health professionals and administrators, and follow your school's protocols.

> **Note:** *This book is not meant to serve as a training or comprehensive resource in suicide assessment or prevention, and it is not meant to supersede any safety protocols already in place at your school. Every professional working with children or young adults should consider attending formal training on how to recognize the warning signs that a student may harm himself or herself or someone else. Some relevant reading materials are listed in the "Resources and Recommendations for Further Reading" section at the end of this book.*

- You suspect that the student is making attempts to hide self-injury, such as wearing only long sleeves (even when this is not appropriate for the weather) or always covering arms with wrist bands or jewelry, or you notice that the student has abrasions in patterns or in unusual places on his body.

- The child's mood problems seem serious, are marked by quick changes, or have existed for an extended period. Trust your instincts. Any dramatic change in attitudes or behaviors warrants communication with school administrators, counselors, or mental health professionals.

- The child confides in you about serious personal problems that are bothering him.

- The student is notably unresponsive to encouragement, positive feedback, or rewards that used to motivate him.

- Caregivers express that they are uncertain where to turn for help in understanding their child's problems. They may need your school's support in connecting with mental health professionals.

Keep in Mind

- You may spend more time observing a child than any other adult outside of his family. If you have concerns, they are worth sharing!

- Although you do not have to take on the role of solving a child's or family's personal problems, you and your school may serve very important roles as conduits to services that can really benefit them.

WHAT TO EXPECT

After class, you tell Justin that you would like to speak with him. His irritation is obvious, but he does stay to see you. You want to let him know that you are concerned about him and want to help, but you are also aware that he may feel more discouraged or embarrassed if too much attention is drawn to his problems. So, you let Justin know that his grade in your class is dropping because he is not finishing his assignments, but you also say that he is very capable of the work and that the expectations will be the same for him. You ask whether he has any ideas for what could help him complete his assignments. Even though you expected him to struggle to come up with possible solutions, asking for his input lets him know that you see him as a competent and valued participant in his education. Knowing that he may have difficulty focusing and thinking optimistically about possible solutions, you suggest that he stop by for just a few minutes every day after school on his way to the bus. At that time, you'll be able to review the homework assignment with him and answer any questions he may have. Justin agrees to do this, but he is very reluctant at first. When he comes into your classroom after school, he acts uninterested and bothered by being there. He also does not show any immediate improvement in completing his assignments. However, you continue to offer support and encouragement, and you make it an expectation that he see you every day for at least a few minutes. Over time, he seems less reluctant to come in to see you and is slightly more engaged. Although there is no dramatic change in his completion of assignments, you are starting to see signs of improvement. Whether these brief meetings help him remember the assignment, increase comprehension of the material, improve his motivation, let him know that you care about him, or just keep you from becoming discouraged, there is some positive effect.

DISCUSSION QUESTIONS

1. As an educator, what are your responsibilities when trying to support students with low moods? What are the limitations of what you can do?

2. What changes should you look for when supporting students with low moods? How will you know whether you are helping?

3. Looking back on your experience, think of a time when you taught a student who may have had a low mood. How did you try to help that student? What else may have been helpful?

4. What protocol are you supposed to follow at your school when you have concerns about a student's safety (e.g., about the potential for suicide)? If you do not have a protocol in place, how could a teacher most effectively communicate his concerns? Whom would you notify first?

5. How can the educators in your school support each other when you suspect that a student is experiencing a low mood?

Strength-Based Goal-Setting Exercise

The objective of this exercise is to help students recognize their personal and academic strengths and how these attributes can be applied to their current schoolwork. The exercise builds positive self-concepts, encourages students to continue striving to succeed, helps educators and students build rapport, and sets specific goals for how a struggling student can get back on track. It is recommended that this exercise be completed or at least reviewed by the student and educator together. You can modify this template to create a form that meets the needs of your specific class or age group.

Fill in the blanks below and review your answers with an adult.

Something I do well (*Choose a talent or strength.*)

_____

_____

How I can use this to succeed in school

_____

_____

My goal (*To start, choose a short-term goal you know you can achieve.*)

_____

_____

My reward (*If you reach your goal, what might be better? How might you feel?*)

_____

_____

Something I do well

_____

_____

How I can use this to succeed in school

_____

_____

My goal

_____

_____

_____

(continued)

Strength-Based Goal-Setting Exercise *(continued)*

My reward

_____

_____

Something I do well

_____

_____

How I can use this to succeed in school?

_____

_____

My goal

_____

_____

My reward

_____

_____

Something I do well

_____

_____

How I can use this to succeed in school?

_____

_____

My goal

_____

_____

My reward

_____

_____

Chapter 4

Refusing School

Miguel has been in your class for 4 months. He is a quiet and polite young man who appears to have two or three friends in class. At the beginning of the school year, you noticed that Miguel had difficulty adjusting to the middle school, which was new to him. He appeared a little timid about engaging in activities. However, with extra encouragement from you and his parents, and some time to get used to his environment, Miguel appeared to acclimate to your class. Outside of an occasional redirection to stay on task, Miguel did not present any significant behavior problems until about 4 weeks ago.

It started with tearfulness at the beginning of the school day but he was able to soothe himself and move forward. Then, you noticed that Miguel's parents were bringing him in tardy to school more often. On arriving to school, Miguel sometimes sat in a corner choking back tears and resisted encouragement to sit in his assigned seat. He reasoned that he could not go along with class activities because his stomach hurt, he was too tired, or he just did not care about the class. Miguel's solution to these problems was that you should let him go home or at least allow him to call his parents.

Miguel's resistance to your encouragement became abrasive at times; he would reject your attention and even support from his friends. You wanted to help soothe his distress, but you also could not spend this much time with him every day because you had other students and lesson plans that required your attention. Further, Miguel needed to understand that he could not act disrespectfully toward his teacher and peers, even if he was upset.

After a few weeks of these escalating difficulties with Miguel, his parents contacted you. They said they were having even more difficulty getting Miguel dressed and ready for school each morning. He protested loudly and with tantrums to avoid school. He made excuses about his teachers being too mean and school being too boring. They knew this was not true. However, like you, they felt pressure to find a solution to Miguel's resistance to school, but they were at wits' end and were not sure what to do.

WHAT YOU MIGHT SEE

- Expressions of fear or insecurity about being away from caregivers
- Reports of extreme fear or discomfort related to attending school
- Crying and tantrums in younger students
- Refusal to participate in class activities, even activities that the student has previously enjoyed
- Physical complaints (e.g., stomachache, headache, nausea) that persist after medical/physiological causes have been ruled out
- Visits to the nurse's office that often occur at certain times of day
- Requests to go home, and presenting these requests as a solution to the complaints
- Frequent requests to call caregivers on the phone and a desire to remain on the phone for extended periods
- Defiance (e.g., "If I can't go home with my mom, then I'm not gonna sit down")
- Aggression, especially when authority figures attempt to persuade compliance

DESCRIPTION OF PROBLEMS

School refusal describes a set of behaviors in which a child attempts to remove himself or herself from academic activities or from the building altogether. Frequently, students will want to return home, have caregivers visit the school, or connect with them on the phone. Students may also want to go to a safe, isolated place, such as the nurse's office or a favorite staff member's office. Refusal behaviors at school are often accompanied by resistance at home. Parents may report that a child uses tantrums, lying, and pleading to avoid school. Students may cling to their parents when they are picked up by the bus or dropped off. Adolescents, in particular, may cut classes, sign parents' names to excuse slips, or even seek suspensions to avoid school and spend time with those with whom they feel close.

Although many children exhibit similar behaviors to accomplish their goals, their motives for doing so may vary. Educators should keep in mind that some students try to avoid school for reasons that are extremely important to them. Negative experiences at school, such as bullying, intimidation, mistreatment by adults, or legitimate medical problems that cause them discomfort during the day, should always be investigated by the appropriate professionals as a first step. Uncomfortable levels of anxiety and fear are often related to refusal behaviors. If an identifiable stressor is influencing a student's resistance to school, then that factor should be addressed before or simultaneously with the refusal behaviors.

Other motivations for resistance to school include insecurity and worry about being apart from loved ones, worry about being away from familiar safe places (e.g., one's home, a friend's home), distress-provoking situations at school (e.g., teasing, academic failure, shyness), perceived rewards (e.g., spending time with friends who also skip school, opportunity to abuse substances), undiagnosed learning problems that make school frustrating, major life changes, or increased recognition and attention from caregivers, educators, and peers. Although some type of worry, insecurity, or emotional need may underlie many students' episodes of school refusal, these factors may not be readily observable, which may perplex parents who struggle to get their child to go to school each day.

Although many students who exhibit resistance to school only do so for relatively brief and fleeting periods, some children may display more severe or persistent refusal behaviors. These more serious episodes of resistance to attending or participating in school can lead to other difficulties if not addressed. When a student feels great distress about being at school, he may act out of character, such as using aggressive behaviors that do not appear in other circumstances. In addition to academic problems caused by missed school, students may develop difficulties with social isolation, discord with parents, or further mood and worry problems.

Because the causes of school refusal can vary greatly and may indicate serious underlying problems that need to be addressed by health care professionals or administrators, this chapter is not meant to substitute for careful assessment and thoughtful interventions by parents and school professionals. However, educators in the classroom often must work with resistant children while underlying problems are being resolved inside or outside of the school. Educators are not always privy to the specifics of the underlying issues, and they must continue to support their students in the classroom the best that they can. To that end, this chapter is intended to provide helpful suggestions.

Recommendations

~~~~~~~~~~~~~~~~ CLASSROOM STRUCTURE ~~~~~~~~~~~~~

Ask Yourself

Is the student's resistance to school made overt (e.g., direct demands to go home), or is the resistance more subtle (e.g., finding reasons to call home frequently or taking the bathroom pass for 25 minutes each class)?

- *Provide boundaries:* If a child is expressing worry about being away from home, it can certainly be appropriate to empathize, support, and soothe that child. It is also important to remind the student that although it is okay to talk about bad feelings and to work with adults to try to solve problems, it is not okay to act disruptively or aggressively to avoid participating in school.

- *Set a time limit:* When helping a student to reduce fussing, complaining, or acting out in apparent efforts to remove himself or herself from school activities, offer the student a time limit on changing his or her behavior (e.g., "Jamie, you have 1 minute before we start class. In 1 minute, you need to become quiet and listen with the rest of the class").

- *Address it early:* Try to address refusal behaviors early before they escalate. For instance, if during a 3-week period an adolescent student seems to be taking the bathroom pass for longer periods of time and appears to be slowly withdrawing from group activities in the classroom, ask the student about this pattern and set limits before the problem becomes more significant.

- *Engage in activities:* Some students will be amenable to distractions or pleasurable activities that help them move past states of worry or distress. Of course, certain students with more serious difficulties will seem incorrigible at times. Nevertheless, the more engaged a student becomes in a role or activity, the more likely that student will be to refocus.

  - Asking a student at the beginning of class to pass out the papers for the day's lesson provides a quick transition into academic activity.

  - If a student calms himself and agrees to sit through morning classes, he can lead a student activity later in the day.

Keep in Mind

- You can show empathy for the distress underlying a student's desire to avoid school, but you should balance your empathy with clear boundaries around acceptable ways for the student to express his distress.

COLLABORATING WITH STUDENTS

Ask Yourself

Has the student ever explained his reasons for wanting to go home or decline participation in class?

Or, does the student propose shifting excuses and behavioral distractions to avoid class?

- *Feel free to ask:* If a student is frequently leaving or missing class but has not actually verbalized a desire to avoid school, consider asking the student whether something is bothering him. Some students are more subtle in their school refusal behaviors and may not verbalize their concerns until they are asked directly.

- *Encourage effective communication:* If the child has difficulty verbalizing the problem or is resistant to considering solutions, leave the door open for future discussion. You might say, "If you think of anything I can do in class to help you feel more comfortable, please let me know." The student's answer might be a first step toward engaging him in class, and it may also help you understand his or her motivation for trying to avoid school.

- *Offer reinforcement for cooperation:* Remember to praise the student for co-operating and sitting through lessons appropriately. Sometimes, we forget to offer attention when a student's behavior returns to what was already expected of him. If one of the child's motivations for school refusal behaviors is to seek recognition, then offering this reinforcement for nondisruptive behaviors will help the student meet his or her needs in an appropriate manner.

Keep in Mind

- Some students' school refusal behaviors can be extremely disruptive to class and frustrating for professionals, such as when a child stands in the back of class and repeatedly demands to go home. However, this sometimes reflects the level of distress the student feels. Your firm but compassionate approach will help balance an understanding of the student with the educational needs of all students.

COLLABORATING WITH THE FAMILY/CAREGIVERS

Ask Yourself

Are the parents aware of the child's resistance to participating in school? Are they also struggling to get the student to go to school each morning?

- *Transition smoothly:* If the student is having difficulty transitioning to school in the morning and clings to parents who are trying to drop him off, it can be helpful to collaborate with parents to create a smooth transition. The details of such a transition will vary depending on the school and the age of the student. However, some possibilities include

- Showing the student that you and his parents trust each other and share the same expectation that he will participate in school; this can be accomplished by letting the student know that you will speak regularly with his parents as long as the problem exists.

- Using similar language when encouraging and setting boundaries for the student around school attendance

- In certain cases, doing an in-person handoff for a few days to help an insecure child feel more trusting of the school environment; this might involve the parent walking a younger child to class and reassuring the child that the teacher will look after him.

- *Work as a team:* Parents, educators, administrators, and school counselors often need to work together to help provide consistent encouragement, reinforcement, and consequences for school refusal behaviors. If you have not yet spoken with the caregivers or other possible members of such a team, consider doing so.

- *Remove reinforcement for absence:* Work with the parents to make sure the student's absence from school is not inadvertently rewarded with games or special attention at home.

- *Chart it:* If you are asking a student to change specific behaviors related to participating in school, it may be helpful to chart the student's progress and share it regularly with parents. This helps improve communication and continuity with the family.

Keep in Mind

- When a student has difficulty explaining what is really bothering him and expresses concerns through indirect means (e.g., excessive complaints about minor issues or myriad excuses to return home), educators may look to parents for answers, and vice versa. The sources of a child's concerns are not always easily detected. In such cases, it is a good idea to involve administrators or other professionals (see next section).

REFERRAL TO AN ADMINISTRATOR, COUNSELOR, OR MENTAL HEALTH PROFESSIONAL

Ask Yourself

Are the child's refusal behaviors escalating or starting to improve?

Has the student expressed a clear reason why he does not want to participate, such as missing his or her parents, being afraid of another student, or expressing excessive self-doubts about being able to accomplish academic tasks?

How are the student's behaviors affecting the class as a whole?

Consider such a step when

- The student's school refusal seems related to a major life stressor that may require additional attention (e.g., bullying, life changes, serious stressors at home, possible medical problems, suspected learning problems).
- The child's behaviors show emotional distress that should be evaluated by a professional.
- The refusal behaviors last more than a week.
- Parents ask for help because severe refusal behaviors at home are clearly affecting the child's ability to attend school and complete homework.
- The student's resistance to school is resulting in significant defiance or aggression.
- Attempts to manage or soothe the student are taking so much time and energy that you are unable to complete lessons or to attend to other students' needs.

Keep in Mind

- Sometimes, resistance to school can be a passing problem that only persists for a week or two. However, if the problem is serious or escalating, a consultation with an administrator or other school professional may be wise. Many school psychologists, social workers, and counselors are trained to help students, teachers, and families manage school refusal behaviors.

WHAT TO EXPECT

While talking with Miguel's parents, you learn that he has recently been to his pediatrician, and no medical concerns were found. You ask whether they are aware of anything outside of school that could be bothering him, such as family changes or stressors in his environment. They say he has not expressed any specific concerns, and they are not aware of anything out of the ordinary in his life outside of school. You tell them that you have checked with his other teachers, and he has not demonstrated any specific academic problems; in fact, when he does his assignments, he does good work. School staff have not identified any other problems that could be contributing to his distress.

Even though the reasons for Miguel's problems in school are not at all clear, you propose a conference with Miguel and his parents. You tell his parents that they seem like a strong source of support and that it may be helpful for Miguel to see everyone working together while also hearing a consistent message about what is and is not acceptable in school.

Children Who Refuse School

Many families have children who refuse school at some point during their education. Although the problem is not uncommon, it can take on many different forms. The severity, duration, and underlying causes of these behaviors can vary greatly. School refusal can occur with children of all ages: from the beginning of formal schooling through the beginning of adulthood.

Is my child refusing school?

There are many ways that children may try to avoid going to school or participating in activities while there. Often, parents and educators notice a pattern in how problems arise to distract a child from attending school. For instance, a younger child may only develop a stomachache during particular classes, or an older child will be absent on test days. Some commonly seen avoidance behaviors include

- Fussing, stalling, or pleading
- Clinging to a caregiver
- Tantrums or crying
- Physical complaints that occur before or during school (headaches or stomachaches)
- Leaving to spend time with friends or be alone during school hours
- Defiance or misbehavior that results in being removed from classes

Why doesn't my child want to go to school?

There are also many different reasons why children avoid school. Some of these reasons can be serious and very important to the child. Others can be resolved more easily with reassurance or a change in daily routine. So, it is wise to carefully consider the possible causes and to talk with school staff about what they have observed before assuming the causes. Some frequent reasons for school refusal include

- Worry and insecurity about being away from family and home
- Worry about interacting socially with peers
- Bullying or mistreatment
- Frustration and disappointment with academic performance (sometimes, children with learning difficulties will avoid classes or activities at which they have felt unable to succeed)
- Reinforcement received for not going to school (getting to spend extra time with family, play video games at home, fit in with peers who also skip school)

(continued)

What should I do to help my child stay at school?

A good place to start is to talk with your child about what is bothering him or her. Have this conversation at a time when your child is calm (not just before school or when reprimanding your child for misbehavior). Sometimes, children will have difficulty explaining what is bothering them, but it is important to ask. Talk to educators or school administrators about your child's behavior when at school. If there is a clear reason that your child may want to stay home, work out a plan to address that underlying issue. Work with school staff so that what you are doing at home and what teachers are doing in school to help your child is as similar as possible. Finally, consider contacting a child therapist if your child is showing significant distress, if the school avoidance has lasted more than a week or two, if you feel unsure how to help, or if you have other serious concerns. Many school districts have counselors, social workers, or psychologists on staff who can support you or provide a referral to a professional in the community.

Chapter 5

Performance Stress

It is not unusual for your students to be nervous before exams. Jaden stands out to you, however, because he is a student who excels in most aspects of your class. His homework assignments are thorough and reflect a high level of comprehension. He has completed several written assignments that have all received high marks. He is conscientious and prompt in completing his work, and he has never presented a behavioral problem in class. In fact, he is rarely absent and seemingly never late for class. Yet, his performance on exams has not reflected the same understanding of the material as shown in other aspects of his work.

As an experienced teacher, you know that each student has strengths and weaknesses in his ability to demonstrate understanding of the material. Some students excel in written work, whereas others demonstrate their knowledge best in small-group activities. Jaden's test scores caught your attention early in the year because they seemed not to match the level of comprehension he demonstrated on his other assignments. Now, several months into the semester, this pattern is becoming even clearer. You are also concerned because Jaden is not just incorrectly answering questions that he seems capable of correctly answering; he is also not finishing his tests. Given his strong work ethic, this does not make sense. Last week, he asked to go to the nurse before an exam, stating that he felt sick to his stomach. You allowed him to go, of course, because he appeared to be in genuine discomfort. You scheduled a makeup time for his test after school the following day, but he did not show for it. With another student, you would not hesitate to treat this as a disciplinary issue. In this case, though, your instincts tell you that Jaden's problems are not simply due to defiance or apathy.

WHAT YOU MIGHT SEE

- Observable anxiety symptoms (e.g., sweating, dry mouth, trembling hands, fidgeting, shortness of breath) when performing a task that entails some element of being evaluated by others or the perception of being evaluated by others
- Performance on certain tasks (e.g., taking tests, participating in class discussion, giving presentations) that is lower than the student's demonstrated abilities on other tasks
- Perfectionism
- Avoidance of, or refusal to engage in certain tasks
- Avoidance of some areas or classes
- Acting-out behavior that results in avoidance of an anxiety-provoking situation (e.g., becoming excessively silly just before a test or becoming disrespectful before speaking in front of the class)
- Physical symptoms (dizziness, headache, upset stomach, light-headedness) that may coincide with specific activities
- A need for support or reassurance around certain activities that is much more than usual for the student

DESCRIPTION OF PROBLEMS

Anxiety is a state of physiological arousal that prepares an individual to react effectively to a demanding situation. Problems with anxiety occur when this physiological state becomes overly intense or emerges in situations that do not require such a response. Performance anxiety revolves around a fear of not meeting one's own standards or the perceived standards of others while performing a task. Therefore, it is usually seen in settings in which individuals are expected to perform tasks in the presence of others. Individuals can experience problems with performance anxiety in situations varying from oral presentations, test taking, or small-group work. Anxiety symptoms can include rapid heartbeat, sweating, dry mouth, dizziness, shortness of breath, light-headedness, trembling, and nausea. In addition, some individuals express somatic (i.e., physical) complaints, such as headaches, fatigue, needing to use the bathroom, or gastrointestinal distress, when experiencing anxiety.

A natural response to anxiety is to avoid the situation that provokes the anxiety so as to regain a sense of calm and well-being. Avoidance is effective in removing the source of stress in the short term, but it often has the effect of worsening the anxiety response in the long term. Severe problems with anxiety usually require treatment through mental health professionals and may involve learning techniques to help manage the anxiety symptoms and make them more tolerable; such problems also may require medications.

Because of the unique demands of the classroom setting, educators may be more likely to see signs of performance anxiety than other adults in a student's life. Teachers play an important role in noticing potential problems with performance anxiety, taking steps to support students in the classroom, and communicating with family members and/or treatment providers. Keep in mind that an individual can have a very specific problem with anxiety, such as performance anxiety, or can have overlapping problems with other types of worry.

Recommendations

~~~~~~~~~~~~~~~~ CLASSROOM STRUCTURE ~~~~~~~~~~~~~~

Ask Yourself

In what ways do I already try to make my classroom a supportive environment for all students? You may already be doing more than you think!

- *Low-key approach:* Remember that the nature of this problem involves fears of being evaluated or negatively judged by others in situations that involve performing a task. Try to minimize the amount of attention drawn to the problem, especially in front of other students.

- *Examine:* Take a fresh look at the classroom environment. Is there any aspect of the environment that could be highlighting these problems for the student? For example, are seating placement, time demands, or group pressure during certain activities worsening the anxiety? Your answers to these types of questions will help you pinpoint how you can best help.

- *Balance:* Helping with this type of anxiety involves a balance between helping to ease the worry and maintaining expectations so as to not contribute to avoidance. Check in with yourself from time to time to see how you are managing this balance. For example, relieving a worried student from all presentations in front of the class, when other students are expected to perform these tasks, may not be the best solution unless this has been recommended by a health professional. This student needs to learn the same speaking skills as his peers. It may be better to be supportive or flexible in helping the student through the task so that he feels a sense of accomplishment at working through a challenge.

- *Address contributing factors:* Be alert to any reactions from peers and/or colleagues that may be contributing to the anxiety. For example, is the child being ridiculed by other students? Could a colleague's attempts at helping actually contribute to the worry? If so, addressing these exacerbating factors may go a long way toward enabling the student to face the tasks.

- *Create a supportive environment:* Encourage students to congratulate their peers' efforts, and remind the class that many people feel nervous about doing a good job or worry about making mistakes in front of others.

Keep in Mind

- Focus on making the classroom as supportive as possible so that the student can engage in academic activities to the best of his abilities. Entirely removing the source of the anxiety will likely worsen the problem in the long run and may prevent the student from learning important skills he will need later in life.

COLLABORATING WITH STUDENTS

Ask Yourself

When did I first notice the problem?

On what tasks does this student perform best? On what tasks does the student seem to struggle?

- *Approach:* Although the problem needs to be addressed, simply doing so might make the student embarrassed or more anxious. Try to use a caring, supportive approach, even though a student's avoidance or resistance to a task can be frustrating.

- *Privacy:* Talk about these problems away from other students to minimize worry about what others might think.

- *Monitor your reaction:* It is natural to want to help someone who is in distress, and, therefore, it can be easy to support avoidance behavior without being aware of doing so. Keep focused on the nature of the problem and the need to provide assistance while not inadvertently supporting avoidance behavior.

- *Maintain expectations:* Demonstrate your belief in the student's ability by keeping up your expectation that all assignments be completed to the best of his ability.

- *Collaborate:* Ask the student for input on what might help manage the anxiety. The student may have ideas but need you to open the lines of communication to feel comfortable expressing them. For example, does the student do or say something to himself that helps him calm down? Does the student have some object that is soothing and helps him feel calm? Does the student have ideas on what would help him or her complete a challenging task, such as taking tests? Sometimes, just having a moment to get a drink of water or use the bathroom before a test can help a student maintain focus.

- *Keep moving forward:* When the student is able to complete a task that causes anxiety, let him know that you recognize this achievement, and keep the positive momentum going!

Keep in Mind

- Demonstrating your care and concern for the student will go a long way toward how your efforts are received. Addressing this problem will naturally move the student away from his comfort zone. Make it clear that you believe in the student and that your goal is to help the student achieve his full potential.

COLLABORATING WITH THE FAMILY/CAREGIVERS

Ask Yourself

What specific observations can I share with the family that highlight this student's strengths and the difficulties he is having?

- *Gather information:* Family members are likely to respect an approach that values their efforts and knowledge. Where have they seen similar problems? What have they tried to help? What has helped, even a little bit? What has not helped or has made the problem worse? When is the child most calm (what is the situation, what is he doing, who is around)?

- *Bridge the gap:* On the basis of what calms or comforts the student at home or in other settings, work with the family to find some small way to bring that comfort into the anxiety-provoking situation in the classroom. For example, if the student feels calm around a sibling, can he bring in a picture of that sibling to look at before a test? Or, if family members say a certain phrase that helps the student feel calm and secure, is there a way to bring that into the classroom to help in times of high anxiety?

- *Emphasize positives:* Although your focus will be on helping with this problem, remember to share with the family positive things the student is doing. Also, make it clear that the problem is not due to lack of effort, ability, or other personal shortcomings.

- *Provide rationale:* Explain to the family that you are keeping up expectations because not doing so would likely make the problem worse over the long run and that it is important for the student to continue learning new skills along with his peers. It is important for the family to understand why the student may feel you are "pushing" him to do something he would rather not do, when you are actually encouraging him to continue growing as a student.

Keep in Mind

- Sharing your direct observations (positive and negative) and getting input from the family demonstrates a nonjudgmental, caring approach that is likely to encourage family participation.

REFERRAL TO AN ADMINISTRATOR, COUNSELOR, OR MENTAL HEALTH PROFESSIONAL

Consider such a step when

- The student is refusing to participate in aspects of class or is consistently avoiding tasks, despite your efforts. In this case, the problem may become so severe that it jeopardizes his chances for academic success.
- You see other problems that could be related to anxiety (e.g., repetitive behaviors, specific fears, frequent physical complaints, social withdrawal).
- The student discloses persistent problems with worry, anxiety, or fear.
- You feel uncertain about how to respond to the student or think that the problem needs more attention.

Keep in Mind

- Trust your instincts. If it is not clear how severe the problem is or whether additional help is needed, it never hurts to consult with others.

WHAT TO EXPECT

You decide to meet with Jaden privately to discuss his difficulty on tests. During your meeting, you are careful not to cause embarrassment or anxiety. You emphasize the high level of his work, and you seek his input about his test performance, adding that taking tests is difficult for many people and is not necessarily related to knowledge of the content. His response indicates frustration and embarrassment. He states that when he gets an exam back and looks at the questions he got wrong, he often knows the right answers. He does not understand why he cannot think of the answers while he is taking the test.

Jaden tells you that, during a test, he thinks a great deal about finishing quickly, and he worries that if he does not turn his test in when others are finished, he will look slow. When you ask him to describe his routine for doing homework, Jaden states that he works in his room, away from his siblings, and does not have to worry about how long he takes to finish. He also tells you that his siblings think of him as a good student and often ask him for help when they have trouble understanding assignments.

From your discussion, it becomes clear that Jaden takes pride in being seen as a good student, and he worries that if he does not finish quickly, others will think poorly of him. As you reflect on the classroom structure, you consider some simple changes. First, instead of having students come up to turn in their exams when they are done, you will ask them to turn their exams facedown and keep them at their desks until the end of the class or the end of the allotted time frame. This will make it less obvious who is or is not finished with the test. You also consider moving Jaden away from a student who sits next to him and finishes her work very quickly. Finally, you will think of ways to allow Jaden to take discreet breaks during the test so that he can take a few moments to relax when he feels stuck. Of course, possible solutions may be limited by the demands of the classroom environment, but your discussion with Jaden and thoughtful reflection on the examination process have created an opportunity for creative adjustments.

DISCUSSION QUESTIONS

1. Have you ever seen an example of performance anxiety? If so, what was your approach, and what happened? What signs of anxiety or worry do you usually look for in your students?

2. What could avoidance look like in your classroom? Would a student be most likely to miss class, go to the nurse, act out, become the class clown, or something else?

3. When you think about your own experiences, recall a time you were worried about what others would think, or think about something that has made you nervous. How did you handle it? What did you do, and what did others do that was helpful?

The following handout is geared toward a middle school through high school age group. For younger students, you can make these suggestions in an age-appropriate manner or provide the handout to parents so that they can reinforce good habits at home.

School Stress

Some of the things we do in school can be pretty stressful.

Taking tests, presenting in front of a class, working with other students on projects, or meeting individually with teachers or principals can all make people feel nervous.

But there are tricks we can use to help keep our bodies and minds calm. Try some of these below:

1. Breathing: Spend a few moments just breathing. Sit comfortably. Let your belly expand as you take a slow breath in, and let the breath out just as slowly as you brought it in (but not so slowly that you make yourself dizzy). Notice a difference? Many people feel more calm after the first breath!

2. Remember your accomplishments: When we feel stressed out, we are usually focusing too much on bad things that could happen (such as failing a test or saying something embarrassing in front of the class). Make a list of successes and accomplishments that you have had. These can include seemingly small successes, such as doing a little better on a test than you expected or finishing a project you thought you'd never get through. Ask a parent, teacher, or friend to name a few more of your accomplishments that they have seen. Take out this list and look at it every once in a while when you are worrying a lot. It might help you feel more confident.

3. Get used to mistakes: Making mistakes is a normal, unavoidable part of life for everyone! Have you ever met a person who didn't make mistakes? That's because there aren't any! Don't be too hard on yourself.

4. Avoid eating or drinking too much of the following when you are stressed out:

   a. Sugar: candy, cookies, soda, etc.

   b. Caffeine: coffee, soda, tea

   Sugar and caffeine can increase your body's reactions to stress; such reactions might include shaky hands or butterflies in the stomach.

5. Exercise: Talk to your family and your doctor about what exercises would be best for you. Regular, moderate exercise can do a lot to help your body and mind de-stress.

Chapter 6

Problems with Authority Figures

Teaching students who test the limits of what they are allowed to do in class is nothing new for you. However, Troy is one of the more challenging students you have taught. He repeatedly pushes the boundaries, and he rarely responds to your redirections in a way that shows respect for you as an adult.

Moreover, when you reinforce class structure or remind him of the rules, Troy ignores you or replies with sarcastic comments. Sometimes, after you ask him to stop a disruptive behavior, he engages in the same behavior just a few minutes later. When you become visibly frustrated by his acting out, he does not seem to have any reaction. Sometimes it even feels like he is encouraged by your frustration. His peers laugh at some of his jokes and surprising behaviors, but many students seem hesitant to become friends with Troy. You have even noticed that when he thinks you are not looking, he sometimes encourages other students to misbehave. It feels like he is competing with you for control of the classroom. How exhausting and distracting!

You have sent Troy to the principal's office several times this year, for such things as speaking disrespectfully to you in front of the class, tipping over his desk when you asked him to clean it, and refusing to leave the room during a fire drill. Troy questions the rules, challenging that his desk is "clean enough," even though it is clearly a mess compared with those of other students. When he refused to leave during a fire drill, he complained that it was pointless to exit the room when there was not a real fire.

You know that your rules and requests are reasonable. Nevertheless, Troy frequently questions your authority, as though applying basic structure in the classroom were arbitrary or oppressive. On the surface, Troy does not appear to have clear reasons for his rule-breaking and authority-challenging behaviors. You have explained the reasons behind the rules, but he shows little interest in trying to see things from anyone else's perspective. The possibility of consequences, such as going to the principal's office, has little impact on him. You worry that his defiant attitudes will become worse as he gets older, making both academics and friendships more difficult for him.

WHAT YOU MIGHT SEE

- Frequently breaks rules or does not follow directions
- Tests limits by seeing what he can get away with before being redirected
- Displays limited regret for disruptive behaviors
- Appears indifferent to the distress adults may show when repeatedly trying to help him follow rules
- May try to get a rise out of adults by not cooperating with them
- Openly questions rules or directions
- Ignores, argues, or laughs when prompted or reprimanded
- Seeks attention from peers by making disruptive comments and jokes during class or by taking on a role as class clown
- May have difficulty establishing close friendships, or gravitates toward other students who act defiantly
- Grades suffer because of limited motivation to achieve good grades or difficulty adhering to assignments and classroom expectations

DESCRIPTION OF PROBLEMS

As with many childhood problems, difficulty respecting the authority of adults and showing disregard for rules and class norms may result from a combination of factors. Contributing factors may include difficulty trusting adults, limited opportunities to see or experience the benefits of following rules, a belief that negative attention is easier to acquire than positive attention, underdeveloped social skills related to making needs known and seeking out assistance in appropriate ways, exposure to inconsistent or overly punitive discipline styles, or feelings of anger and resentment toward people in positions of power.

Because this type of behavior seems to cause the individual and those around him tremendous problems, it can be difficult to remember that all behavior is learned because it is (or was) effective in some situations. And, just as behavior is learned over time, it changes over time. Problems with authority and rules can be particularly slow to change because other, more useful skills may not have been developed to fall back on.

Problems with authority can be associated with aggressive behavior, emotional distress, poor academic and social adjustment, future problems with the legal system, and future employment difficulties.

Recommendations

~~~~~~~~~~~~~~~~ CLASSROOM STRUCTURE ~~~~~~~~~~~~~~~~

Ask Yourself

Is it what the student is saying or how is saying it that challenges the rules and your role as teacher?

What are three specific behaviors that the student would benefit from changing?

What is this student doing well?

- *Behaviors may get worse (before they get better):* When a pattern of behavior is challenged by a change in the rewards and consequences that existed previously, a child or adolescent often tries harder to get the same results as before. For example, if the student feels as though he is receiving less attention for questioning class rules and is receiving more consistent consequences without debate, the student may initially increase his attempts to debate you. However, after a period of time, the student will recognize that he cannot entice you into debate, will learn to predict the consequences, and will decrease these disruptive behaviors.

- *Experiment with seating:* Although it is important to have a student sit in a place where his behaviors can be easily observed, some students who are placed in the front-center of the room use the opportunity to impress an audience of classmates by further challenging the teacher. Some defiant students will act out less frequently if they are placed a few rows back or to the side of the room, where they feel less stimulated.

- *Watch for disruptive subgroups:* A student may join in with the negative behaviors of peers or actively attempt to pull others into his or her negative behaviors. Be proactive if you think this is happening—as needed, help to buffer between students by asking them to sit apart from each other or keeping them occupied with productive activities. It may be helpful to explain that this is not a punishment but, instead, a way to help them each focus on class material.

~~~~~~~ COLLABORATING WITH THE FAMILY/CAREGIVERS ~~~~~~~

Ask Yourself

How do the student's authority-challenging statements and behaviors impede his or her learning in class?

Have the parents received feedback from other educators, or will this be new information to them?

- *Call when you feel calm:* We all know how frustrating and upsetting it can be when a child repeatedly acts rude or defiant when you are trying to teach the child and help him grow. However, if you need to call home, parents may be most receptive to your concerns if they perceive that your approach is calm and thoughtful. If you feel upset but need to call the student's parents, first take a 10-minute breather. You probably deserve it!

- *Do not judge character:* Keep your feedback focused on specific behaviors, and be cautious not to generalize about personality flaws. Remember that the child may feel picked on when he receives consequences for his negative behaviors, and the child may express this to his support network. Be clear with the family that you only want the best for their child and that learning to follow directions and respect legitimate authority figures will benefit the child throughout his life.

- *Remind them that it is not about you:* It can be helpful for parents to be reminded that, as an educator, part of your role is to encourage effective academic and social behaviors. You do not punish students because they offend you; rather, you direct students toward behaviors that will help them reach their goals in life.

- *Share what works:* Consider sharing with the parents the interventions that have worked or not worked in the classroom to help the student remain cooperative. Ask the parents whether they have any pointers regarding what helps their child accept directions or limits.

- *Use written communication:* Brief notes on calendars or behavior-tracking sheets help keep the parents involved and apprised of current issues in the classroom.

- *Identify strengths:* Children who present with frequent authority-challenging behaviors may often land themselves in trouble, drawing much attention to their problems. Sometimes, a child's problems seem to greatly overshadow his or her strengths. As when communicating with the child, remind the caregivers of the positive skills that the student also demonstrates.

Keep in Mind

- Parents sometimes benefit from encouragement, too.
- Demonstrating your concern for the student will go a long way.

REFERRAL TO AN ADMINISTRATOR, COUNSELOR, OR MENTAL HEALTH PROFESSIONAL

Ask Yourself

How long has the student displayed these behaviors?

How effective have classroom interventions been?

Have you noticed anything else of concern besides the challenging or defiant behaviors?

Consider such a step when

- You are aware that the child's defiant, disruptive behaviors are evident across multiple classes and settings. When a child's functioning is inhibited in multiple areas of life, more intensive intervention may be warranted.

- The student's pattern of defiance is relatively new and arose suddenly, marking a noticeable change in his attitude and demeanor.

- The child is significantly disrupting the classroom learning environment for himself and for his peers.

- The student's challenging behaviors are accompanied by mood swings, frequent crying, isolation, or aggression. Some children act out when they are experiencing mood problems because they do not have the words to express what is really bothering them.

- You feel exhausted and unsure about what will work to help the student. Sometimes, a consultation with another professional can benefit both you and the student.

Keep in Mind

- There are often a number of reasons the student is demonstrating these behaviors in your classroom. If your interventions are not successful, do not hesitate to consult with other professionals. It is likely that the lack of response indicates the complexity and severity of the problem.

WHAT TO EXPECT

After taking some time to evaluate where to start with Troy, you prioritize the issues you would first like to address. At the top of your list are completing assignments and not disrupting the class through inappropriate behavior or statements. As you reflect on when he refuses assignments or disrupts the class, you notice that he is often successful in pulling you into discussions or debates about the importance of the assignment or the material being presented. As a conscientious teacher, it is important to you to help students understand the relevance of the material you teach. In this case, however, Troy has discovered a way to

Parent–Teacher Communication Sheet

Goals

To reduce (problem behaviors):

To increase (positive behaviors):

In school today _____
                    (name)

Problem behavior(s)

	Rarely	Sometimes	Often	Very often
	Rarely	Sometimes	Often	Very often

Positive behavior(s)

	Rarely	Sometimes	Often	Very often
	Rarely	Sometimes	Often	Very often

Teacher comments:

      What to focus on tomorrow:

Parent comments:

Chapter 7

Fitting in with Peers

Despite Jane's resilient efforts to develop a group of friends, you have watched her struggle with this all year. She is not shy about starting conversations, but, before long, the other kids are drifting away back to solitary activities or moving to talk with different peers. This can be difficult to watch because Jane is well meaning and sincere in trying to fit in. However, something just has not clicked between her and the other students. It is tough to identify the problem from a distance. Perhaps, Jane is a little too stilted, her jokes are a bit awkward, or her timing is off. All you know for sure is that she has been experiencing a lot of rejection.

When Jane's attempts to connect with peers do not work, she gravitates toward you and other adults in the school who are more accepting of her. This is okay with the staff. Jane is a pleasure to teach, but it does not seem healthy for her to substitute interactions with adult staff in place of peer relationships. You and colleagues who also have Jane in classes hope that her unique social style will someday be better received by peers, but, at this age, she is really struggling to be accepted.

WHAT YOU MIGHT SEE

- Spending time alone while others are interacting
- Frequent attempts to socialize that appear rejected by peers
- An apparent lack of effort to socialize (which could be due to frequent rejections and self-doubt)
- Hesitance or nervousness to engage with other students

- Behaviors that demonstrate less developed social skills or awareness of how others respond to them
- Spending more time with adults, much older students, or much younger students (these are not necessarily problems in and of themselves, but they sometimes reflect social difficulties)
- Self-deprecating statements that reflect a low self-opinion, particularly as it relates to how others may view him or her

DESCRIPTION OF PROBLEMS

Precocious qualities, which are strengths in one sense, can also be limiting because other children might find them difficult to relate to. Ironically, these precocious characteristics are sometimes the same ones that help students become successful as adults (e.g., a devoted focus on a subject of interest, a strong sensitivity to how others feel, a talent for relating better to adults, a serious demeanor).

For certain children, school feels like an artificial arrangement in which they are constantly put in social situations that make them feel uncomfortable or that are simply not interesting to them. Nevertheless, they experience pressure to conform because isolation is also unpleasant, and peer pressure to fit in can be enormous. For other children, social interactions at school are of tremendous interest, and they would love to have friends. However, they are rejected frequently, often without understanding why they cannot fit in. These experiences can be painful. Many adults have their own stories of how difficult and confusing it was to experience rejection as children.

Sometimes, children cannot change and, perhaps, should not change aspects of their personalities that make it more difficult to fit in. However, learning new social skills, developing greater awareness of how others interpret their behaviors, and having situations in which to practice new skills can relieve some of the social stress. When problems fitting in exist for prolonged periods, children can develop negative beliefs about themselves, low moods from disappointment and rejection, and isolation. They may also become more vulnerable to risky behaviors to cope with social problems or to try to gain status among peers.

Recommendations

~~~~~~~~~~~~~~ CLASSROOM STRUCTURE ~~~~~~~~~~~~~~

Ask Yourself

Do my classroom activities foster positive interactions among students?

Does the structure of my class offer opportunities for collaboration and strength building beyond the academic subject at hand?

- *Create opportunities:* Students who are working to develop social skills often benefit from increased opportunities to practice in a more structured context. In school, this might include group projects of various kinds, both inside and outside of class.

- *Demonstrate the skills:* When chances arise, demonstrate effective social skills for the class. For instance, if three students are working together on an activity and all are exhibiting respect toward each other or they successfully work through a conflict, you might ask them to briefly describe to the rest of the class how they accomplished this. Fostering an atmosphere in which students are learning about managing relationships as well as academics will increase their sensitivity to how they treat and include each other.

- *Emphasize tolerance:* Remind the class to appreciate differences of all kinds. Helping a student feel accepted is as much about the rest of the class developing more mature social skills as it is about the one child finding ways to fit in. Children with trouble making friends sometimes ask or, at least, wonder, "What is wrong with me?" From an adult perspective, the answer may be, "Absolutely nothing." A primary reason why some individuals are left out is that the other children are still developing their own senses of acceptance and respect for differences of opinion, attitude, and characteristics.

- *Praise efforts:* When many students are showing attitudes of acceptance and tolerance toward each other, make your observations known. By offering general praise, you are not publicly identifying any children who might be struggling to fit in, which could cause embarrassment. Rather, you are setting an expectation for how students will treat each other, and you are indirectly making it easier for those who feel left out.

Keep in Mind

- Because skills for working collaboratively and developing positive rapport with peers is important in most career and leisure activities, emphasizing these skills among children can help them foster successful application of academic subjects later in life.

COLLABORATING WITH STUDENTS

Ask Yourself

Has this student asked for help? How could I help normalize the student's difficulties and encourage the student to feel good about himself or herself regardless of his or her struggles?

- *Build on strengths:* Take notice of what the child already does well in her efforts to get along with others. Let the child know that you see this ability in her, and encourage the child to feel good about it.

- *Offer options:* Rather than pushing a shy or nervous child into interactions that might make her feel uncomfortable, consider offering it as a choice that you support. For example, you could suggest that Jane sit with another girl at lunch who often sits alone, that they could both join another table of students, or that Jane could consider these options tomorrow.

- *Put it in context:* If the student is struggling and expresses frustration, remind her that many people go through periods of loneliness or rejection. If you know of someone the child admires who has talked about struggling to fit in, you could mention it. There are many successful and famous people who have talked about their status as "nerds" or "rejects" while growing up.

- *Practice acceptance:* By overtly showing that you do not judge or think any less of a child who feels different, you are already providing a useful intervention. (You probably demonstrate this naturally all the time.) Youth can sense those attitudes from you, even if they are not spoken, and it can feel very supportive.

- *Provide the long view:* It is difficult for people to see beyond elementary, middle, or high school when they are young. However, there is a big world with lots of opportunities to find people and social activities as an adult. It can help to remind young people of this.

Keep in Mind

- Many students may feel insecure even discussing social problems with an adult. The more calm and comfortable you are discussing problems fitting in, the more the student will feel at ease. These really are not problems to be ashamed of, anyway; there are many successful people who describe having felt rejected throughout childhood.

COLLABORATING WITH THE FAMILY/CAREGIVERS

Ask Yourself

Are the caregivers seeing a problem that you do not see, or vice-versa? What might be the benefit of speaking with them about this student's difficulty fitting in with others?

- *Normalize, but do not minimize:* Many children go through periods of social turmoil or difficulty adjusting to new groups of peers, and not all young people need to be socialites. Some children simply do not feel the need to have more than two or three friends, who in some cases might be cousins or siblings. However, if a child is disturbed by the situation, or if concerned adults recognize a larger problem, then there are plenty of resources, groups, books, professionals, and other ways to improve the situation.

- *Take the temperature:* Talk with the parents about how their son or daughter is reacting to the situation. The child's reaction will help you all to gauge the seriousness of the situation. Some children with similar difficulties may seem deeply bothered, whereas others hardly seem fazed.

- *Share your knowledge:* You may remind the parents that sadness and disappointment are not necessarily the reactions the child will present. Withdrawal, clinginess, irritability, and lack of interest in going to school are other ways that children express their responses to rejection or isolation. Conversations about how school is going are important, particularly for more reticent children.

- *Develop a plan:* If you and the family decide that action needs to be taken to support the student, then consider interventions that can be reinforced both at home and in school. Examples might include

  - A parent teaches his daughter a new social skill each week and lets the educator know that she will practice it in school. The educator then praises her when she employs this skill in school.

  - The teacher and caregivers identify activities that will help boost the student's confidence. The adults then work together to create opportunities and to encourage these confidence-building activities both in and out of school.

Keep in Mind

- Consistent interventions across settings (school and home) create faster and longer-lasting change.

REFERRAL TO AN ADMINISTRATOR, COUNSELOR, OR MENTAL HEALTH PROFESSIONAL

Ask Yourself

How long have you noticed these problems for this student?

How does the student respond to the problems?

Has the child asked for help?

Consider such a step when

- The student's social struggles appear chronic, that is, they persist across different settings for weeks, months, or years.

- The student appears markedly distressed by rejections or isolation.

- There are co-occurring problems in academic performance, mood (e.g., irritability or sullenness), or stress level.

- Trouble fitting in seems related to aggressive behaviors, such as making fun of or intimidating other students.

- The student expresses interest in learning how to get along better with others.

Keep in Mind

- Although some rejection and periods of decreased social interaction occur in most people's lives, interventions for youth who struggle more seriously with these issues can have long-lasting positive impacts.

WHAT TO EXPECT

As you assign a structured, small-group project with aspects to be completed in and outside of class, you carefully select students for Jane's group who are most likely to accept her. For this assignment, each group member will be expected to introduce a subject of interest to his or her group partners and then integrate that subject into a group presentation. You suspect that this format will allow Jane a structured way to relate to her peers through sharing one of her interests. As students work on this project in class, you make sure to praise students you see helping peers and working in respectful ways with each other.

Jane has always sought you out individually; she appears more comfortable with you and other adults than with her peers. When others are not around, you make an extra effort to reflect her strengths and positive qualities. You also look for opportunities to gently let her know that learning how to relate to others can be very difficult and that many people have gone through times when they do not feel well liked by others. Knowing that Jane has a strong interest in singing, you mention how you heard a popular singer talking about having a hard time in school and not having many friends. Jane, of course, is very familiar with this singer, and she is excited to comment on how famous the singer is and how many friends she must have now.

At your next teacher–parent conference, you ask Jane's family whether they have noticed Jane having a hard time relating to and being accepted by peers. They state that she has extended family members whom she plays with but that she has no friends from school. They first suspected a problem when they asked her whom she would like to invite to her birthday party; she became irritable and seemed like she did not want to answer. Jane's parents tell you that they are working with her on listening to others because they have noticed that she has a hard time listening to them in conversations and often interrupts because she is eager to say something. Knowing this, you tell her parents that you can look for times when she is listening well to you or one of her peers and that you will help to reinforce such positive behavior.

DISCUSSION QUESTIONS

1. Why is socialization an important part of a child's academic development? What social skills are important for academic and professional success?

2. When do common experiences of minor rejection start to become more significant problems in a child's development?

3. Why is it important for children who have different interests or different ways of interacting to feel good about their differences and to feel free to not fit in, if they prefer?

4. What are some ways you have helped children integrate better with their peers? What worked well, and what did not work?

The following are suggestions for how you can integrate social skills training into your typical academic activities. Remember that a student's ability to fit in with peers is not just about that individual's difficulties with social skills or superficial differences that seem to result in exclusion. It is also about the ability of other students to learn mature ways of managing differences and to develop a "big picture" understanding of how important it is for everyone to feel included and respected.

---

*   Include both small-group and large-group exercises in your learning activities. Different-sized groups involve different interpersonal dynamics and skills for those involved.

*   Rotate leadership positions. Make sure that every student has an opportunity to take on prominent roles in the classroom. These roles should be sufficiently structured so that students with varying abilities to make decisions and manage behavior can succeed. Not only is it helpful for students who do not fit in as well to experience being leaders, it is equally beneficial for other students to see and respect them in these positions.

*   For some activities, provide everyone with a role or have them come up with their own designations within work groups. This helps them think in a larger social context (e.g., everyone contributes to the whole).

*   Emphasize tolerance for different opinions, and foster discussions about subjects on which students might disagree. Learning to respectfully disagree is a skill that can benefit a person throughout life.

*   Include active listening skills in group assignments. Active listening involves not only ensuring that you have accurately heard your peer but also acknowledging to the peer that she was heard. Body language is as important as verbal communication.

Chapter 8

Aggression

Maria is a student in your fifth-grade class. She enjoys being the center of attention and can be quite charming. However, you are aware that she is frequently in trouble at school and has regular meetings with the school counselor and other professionals in the community.

Since the beginning of the year, you have addressed some of Maria's challenging behaviors, such as pushing items off her desk, throwing objects in the room, yelling, and banging her desk with her hands. These behavior incidents are very disruptive to your classroom, but afterward Maria seems remorseful and shows a desire to work on assigned activities. Less frequently, she has pushed and threatened other students. She once made a verbal threat toward you when you attempted to set limits with her in the middle of an outburst. The other students appear somewhat fearful of her. They are receptive when she initiates interaction, but they do not seek out her company.

Maria's other teachers report similar problems in their classes. Your colleagues have tried various methods, but none have seen lasting improvements. Maria has outside professionals working with her, but you are not sure exactly what strategies they are using. As Maria's difficulties worsen, school administrators consider developing an individualized education program.

WHAT YOU MIGHT SEE

- Physical aggression, such as hitting, pushing, kicking, or spitting
- Threatening or intimidating physical postures, such as raising a fist, standing over a seated peer, glaring stares

- Verbal aggression, such as yelling, swearing, name calling, or threatening

- An identifiable cause of the aggressive behavior may be readily apparent, or the behavior may appear to be "out of the blue."

- May be well liked by peers (not necessarily associated with peer rejection)

- May have negative attitudes toward school

- Other types of treatment providers may be involved in meetings about the student, classroom observations, and so forth.

- The student may have formalized plans or guidelines put into place by school personnel (school counselor/psychologist or other team members)

DESCRIPTION OF PROBLEMS

Some students who demonstrate aggressive behavior might only do so in certain situations, such as in response to a specific, unwanted demand. Other students exhibit aggressive behavior in a variety of contexts as part of a larger set of problems involving frequent violations of the rights of others. An individual may engage in a very narrow range of aggressive behavior (e.g., only verbal threats) or a broad range of aggressive behavior (e.g., threats, posturing, angry stares, throwing objects, fighting). With some students, this behavior may be seen as controlled and calculated, and with other students it may seem more volatile and impulsive.

The causes of aggressive behavior are often multidimensional and challenging to accurately assess. Aggressive behavior can be used as a way to achieve a desired outcome, such as avoidance of a particular task, or it can be the result of poor frustration tolerance and limited behavioral control. Often, there are several reasons for the aggressive behavior, which may involve biological, psychological, and social factors. Because of the potential complexity of the underlying causes of aggressive behavior, hasty or overly simplistic explanations (e.g., "She is doing it for attention") are likely inaccurate or only partially accurate.

Regardless of the cause of the aggressive behavior, it should be considered a serious problem that will interfere with many aspects of the student's life if it persists. It also will undoubtedly affect peers who are exposed to it. Aggressive behaviors are associated with problems in academic achievement, social development, self-esteem, and emotional well-being. In some cases, aggressive behavior precedes association with a negative peer group, substance abuse, and involvement in the legal system.

Recommendations

~~~~~~~~~~~~~~~ CLASSROOM STRUCTURE ~~~~~~~~~~~~~~~

Ask Yourself

What safety concerns do you have (either for other students or yourself)?

Is there anything about the environment of the classroom that increases risk, such as heavy/sharp objects or breakable glass equipment?

- *Prevention:* Focus your effort on prevention because this is the area in which you are most likely to be effective. After an aggressive outburst, especially one that involves physical violence, you should follow your school's safety procedures and disciplinary process.

- *Know warning signs:* Use your keen observation to become aware of the pattern of aggressive behavior. What happens in the days and hours leading up to the behavior? What happens right before the behavior? What changes did you notice in the student's demeanor or attitudes? What changes occurred in the environment? What were her interactions with other students like? What interactions did you have with the student before an act of aggression?

- *Stay the course:* Remain consistent in your approach and your interventions with the student in your classroom. Work as a team member with other professionals who may be involved with the student; consistency across classes and between home and school will contribute to positive results.

- *Connect:* Although the aggressive behavior is likely your most pressing concern (and rightfully so), make a conscious decision to get to know the student. Find out what interests and motivates the student, what captures her attention, and to what she responds. The relationship you build during times of calm will be an important tool when attempting to divert acts of aggression.

- *Teamwork:* Remember that aggressive behavior is a complex and difficult problem that is best managed by a team of professionals. Discuss the concerns you are having in your classroom with other teachers and administrators. Look for similarities and differences in their observations and yours.

- *Plan ahead, and use your resources:* If aggressive behavior disrupts your classroom, consider working with colleagues to move your students to another location. Prepare for this ahead of time by being ready with needed materials and talking with your colleagues about how to coordinate such a response. Although this may be an inconvenience for the rest of your class, maintaining the safety of all students is the highest priority.

- *Support your other students:* Provide praise and encouragement to students who are exposed to a peer's aggressive behaviors but who do not imitate or use that peer's example as a justification to act out themselves. Be attentive to the feelings and sense of safety of students after they have witnessed an act of aggression. For some, witnessing such an event can be as troubling as being the target of the hostility. Witnesses may also require a referral to speak with a school counselor or administrator for additional support.

Keep in Mind

- Both verbal and physical aggression by students can be upsetting to witness and are a drain on your time, energy, and other resources. Be sure to take care of yourself, too. If you are feeling burned out, plan some restful activities and share your thoughts and feelings with a trusted colleague or friend. If you work in a school with frequent violence or the threat of violence, you are also subject to chronic stress. This can creep up on you over weeks or months.

～～～～～ COLLABORATING WITH STUDENTS ～～～～～

Ask Yourself

Does the student's aggression build up over minutes or hours, or does it suddenly appear?

How do you feel teaching this student?

How do you feel when her behavior becomes hostile or disruptive?

- *Strike while the iron is cold:* The best time to discuss these issues with a student is when she is calm. Once a child is wound up, discussion and reasoning may be less effective. At that point, you should consider using de-escalation skills that have been determined effective for that student, briefly stating clear expectations, and using other methods, such as providing diversions or modifying the classroom structure.

- *Do not expect explanations:* Be aware that the student may not be fully aware of why she shows aggression. It is certainly okay to ask, but it is not uncommon for young people to be unsure why they act out. Sometimes, they wish they could stop and feel bewildered by their own actions. Understanding the reasons behind aggression is likely to involve an evaluation that includes information from a number of different sources (the student, colleagues, parents, health care professionals, etc.).

- *Observe your reactions:* Feelings such as fear, helplessness, and anger are a normal reaction to someone else's aggressive behavior. Be aware of any emotional reaction you are having, and use your support system to help you manage these feelings. By doing so, you will put yourself in a position to work more effectively with the student.

- *Maintain expectations:* Set clear and consistent limits, but maintain a calm and compassionate manner. By doing so, you are modeling appropriate assertiveness, which is likely to be an underdeveloped skill for the aggressive child.

- *Describe what you see:* When talking with the student, focus on what you have directly observed and how this affects school performance for the individual as well as other students in the class. Keep a pragmatic approach and avoid labeling or quickly assuming causes for the behavior. Such an approach will help to minimize defensiveness.

- *Be alert and decisive:* When you see warning signs, act immediately. Attempt to engage the student in some other activity, but emphasize that the purpose of doing so is to help her transition back to classroom expectations.

- *Provide a positive role:* Remember that a student who engages in aggressive behavior may be lacking in basic social skills and self-esteem. The student may also lack a clear sense of a role among her peers other than as a troublemaker or some other negative identity. By attempting to find positive, unique roles for the student (e.g., in charge of leading a class discussion or passing out papers on a certain day), you are helping the student develop a healthy sense of self and find a way to fit in with classroom expectations in a meaningful and productive way.

- *Keep focused on goals:* Remember to stay aware of the goals the student is working toward because it is easy to focus only on the behavior you want the student to avoid. Work with the student to set small, realistic, achievable goals that are incompatible with aggressive behavior. Each time a goal is met, provide praise and verbal reinforcement.

Keep in Mind

- Children with severe problems such as aggressive behavior sometimes appear like they do not care about praise or encouragement. Remember that this can stem from a need to seem tough, the presence of significant insecurity and self-doubt, or uncertainty as to how to internalize or respond to these statements. So, do not lose hope, stay consistent, and remember that positive reinforcement is more effective in changing behavior than is punishment.

COLLABORATING WITH THE FAMILY/CAREGIVERS

Ask Yourself

What are the student's parents/caregivers likely to be concerned about when they receive calls regarding their child's aggression?

What ideas do I have for how to manage this behavior in my classroom, and how can the family help support that plan?

- *Show your concern:* Approach the family with concern for them and the student. Although you may have witnessed acts of aggression or even been the victim of aggressive behavior, try to stay objective and focused on your concern for the student. Show interest in the hardship this behavior is causing them (embarrassment, shame, legal problems). This will go a long way because they may be used to being blamed.

- *Start with positive assumptions:* Work from the assumption that the caregivers want the best for their child, are very concerned about the problem, and are willing to work with you to address the behavior. It is common to presume that a severe behavior problem must be related to poor parenting or indifferent caregivers, but it is more likely that the caregivers are struggling themselves with how to manage the behavioral problems. Your nonjudgmental approach will help to build a collaborative working relationship.

- *Report facts:* Share the specific problems you are observing in your class. Remember that your primary focus is on specific problems in your classroom rather than on addressing larger family issues or seeking explanations.

- *Seek input:* Ask the caregivers about their concerns and their ideas for improving the situation.

- *Offer to work with the team:* If the caregivers mention other professionals working with the child, offer to speak directly to those individuals to help coordinate the child's care (guardians will probably need to provide written permission to those people).

Keep in Mind

- Showing an understanding that the child's behaviors may be upsetting or perplexing to the family can make it easier for them to collaborate with school staff.

REFERRAL TO AN ADMINISTRATOR, COUNSELOR, OR MENTAL HEALTH PROFESSIONAL

Ask Yourself

Is this student posing a danger to himself or herself or to others?

Is her aggression escalating in severity?

Consider such a step when

- The problem involves direct threats, physical violence, or a pattern of more mild aggressive behavior that disrupts your ability to teach. Always follow your school's policies for safety and disciplinary measures.

- You are concerned about the student being hurt outside of your classroom or outside of school. Even if you do not have clear evidence, it does not hurt to talk out your concerns with a school counselor or administrator.

If the student does have professionals in place, keep open communication with them (assuming the student's guardians have signed consent for those people to talk with you). Your efforts will be appreciated because you observe the child more than almost anyone else, and the success of any behavioral intervention is dependent on consistency across settings. In other words, your involvement is critical to the success of a comprehensive treatment program.

Remember that with a problem as severe as this, you should see yourself as a member of a team of professionals who are working with the student and the family. You are an integral part of this team, but do not feel like you can solve this problem on your own.

Keep in Mind

- Because verbal and physical violence can have a strong impact on many people, it never hurts to get a second opinion or to broaden the network of adults who can support the student.

WHAT TO EXPECT

After a particularly challenging day with Maria, you decide to contact her guardians. Her mother starts off by telling you all the efforts she is making to help Maria. You let her know that she is doing a great deal to help Maria, and your hope is that working with her will help Maria in your classroom. It is important to communicate that your concern is for Maria, not for finding blame or seeking punishment. You share with her two recent observations of Maria that illustrate your biggest concerns. Maria's mother tells you that Maria is receiving professional services outside of school, and they are planning a meeting with the school counselor. She invites you to attend and states that she will provide Maria's counselor with permission to include you in this meeting.

In preparation for the meeting, you start keeping track of when Maria is engaging in safe behavior and when her behavior is aggressive or threatening. You keep track of details such as the time of day that incidents occur, the scheduled activity at that time, what is going on in the immediate environment, any significant peer or staff interactions before an incident, and any changes in Maria's behavior or demeanor before an incident.

When Maria is not engaging in aggressive behavior, you make it a priority to point out and praise her specific behaviors. When she is calm, you also privately remind her of safety rules in the classroom, and you explain why these are important. You also make a point to emphasize in these discussions how her current behavior demonstrates adherence to these safety rules.

Preparing for the meeting with Maria's treatment providers has made you very aware of the important role you play in helping Maria and of the need for everyone involved to be working on an integrated and well-coordinated plan.

DISCUSSION QUESTIONS

1. What is aggression? Must it include hurtful words or physical acts, or can it include subtler behaviors?

2. In your experience, how have aggressive students affected the learning of peers?

3. Do you work in a school in which aggressive acts often occur inside the building? Have news stories about violence in schools affected how you think about your workplace? If so, how do you deal with this?

The following exercise can be used with an entire class or with a small group of students who are showing problems with aggression. You can modify it to suit your particular class or age group. The approach is designed to build awareness of aggression and what the realistic consequences are for the aggressor and for those who are impacted.

AGGRESSION IN SCHOOL: WHY IT IS A BIG DEAL

Depending on your students' age range and time availability, you can begin this activity by setting up a brief skit demonstrating a form of aggression that might occur in class or a subtle form that will spark disagreement about whether it actually is aggression or not.

Ask the Student(s)

What is aggressive behavior?

Allow your students to explain, and then provide feedback. Sample definition: It can be hitting, pushing, yelling, taking something from someone's hands, name calling, or other actions that hurt, frighten, or intimidate others.

How does it affect you if someone acts aggressively toward you?

Allow them to explain, and then provide feedback. Sample responses include hurt feelings, fear, or not wanting to be around that person.

If you use aggression, does it help you get what you want? What do you get?

Allow them to explain, and then provide feedback. Some may chime in and say that it absolutely does get them a place in line, attention from friends, status in school, an extra snack, etc., and that is right to a point. You can catch the students off guard by agreeing that it might sometimes help them get what they want…but then ask them to follow this logical thought process through.

Other than occasionally helping you get what you want, what else do you get? What are the negative consequences?

Students with aggressive behaviors will often need help and encouragement to follow through with this chain. The idea is to go beyond just disciplinary consequences and to really examine what happens when someone acts with aggression. Ask the students to brainstorm more ideas than is easy for them. If they are giving few answers, ask them to come up with 10 or 15 responses. You can write them on the board.

Examples

- Some students do not want to be around you.
- Peers are more likely to show fear or avoidance than respect or appreciation toward you.
- If you are having a bad day, other students are less likely to ask you about it or to try to help if they think you might be mean to them.
- Family may be disappointed (if not in the aggression itself, then in the suspension, detention, distraction from academics, etc.).
- Of course, there also might be disciplinary consequences.

Do people think about all of these consequences before they act aggressively toward others? What do they think about?

Allow them to explain, and then provide feedback.

What would happen if you chose not to use aggression in a frustrating situation?

Allow them to explain, and then provide feedback. Encourage the students to focus on how they actually benefit by not using aggression. Help them weigh the benefits of acting out versus not acting out. Help steer the discussion to allow students to recognize that the short-term gratification of aggressively acting backfires by substituting short-term gratification for a variety of negative outcomes.

Chapter 9

Students Who Are Bullied

Jonathan is a typical student in one of your afternoon classes. Sometimes, he talks during lessons and acts goofy on Fridays—nothing out of the ordinary. He often carries a saxophone case with him because he is involved with the school music program. He has also mentioned that he takes private lessons. Overall, Jonathan's academic marks are a little above average.

A few months ago, you heard that Jonathan was in a small shoving match in the hall. The event was handled by staff, and Jonathan's year continued without further incident. It was not a major topic of discussion because it was a relatively small disciplinary event. However, Jonathan does not seem like the type to become physically aggressive, so you presumed he did not instigate it.

Recently, you noticed that Jonathan was carrying his instrument case less frequently to class. He also started to seem less animated and talkative. However, this was not particularly alarming because it might have reflected a normal fluctuation in a young person's mood. Then, yesterday, Jonathan arrived in class late with a grass stain on his jeans, ruffled hair, and a sour look on his face. You overheard another student in class joking about what a few peers had done to Jonathan earlier in the day, but you did not catch the details. When you asked Jonathan what had happened, he seemed upset but said it was "no big deal."

WHAT YOU MIGHT SEE

Common forms of bullying include teasing; insulting; name calling; mimicking; ostracizing; making inappropriate remarks related to sex, race, culture, or identity issues; touching in ways that are unwelcome; physically assaulting; or otherwise acting to make a peer(s) feel degraded.

The bullied student might

- Spend less time around other children or cling to those who make him feel safe
- Display mood changes, which can be acute or prolonged
  - Sudden tearfulness, fear, sullenness, or anger, particularly after an incident of bullying
  - An overall decline in mood or functioning in school and other activities
- Make self-deprecating remarks (which reflect the harassing slights of others)
- Show physical marks, such as redness on skin, bruises, torn bookbag, or dirt or food on clothing
- Attempt to cover up a physical feature or other characteristic (e.g., way of talking or acting) that others have ridiculed

DESCRIPTION OF PROBLEMS

In this chapter, *bullying* is defined as a broad category of harassment that includes intimidation, ridicule, deliberate exclusion, threats, hitting, spitting, pushing, and many other forms of degradation. The content of such degradation may involve targeting victims on the basis of their race, ethnicity, gender, sexual orientation, language, social skills, physical characteristics and abilities, or intellectual or emotional capacities. Sometimes, young people are targeted for reasons as seemingly arbitrary as what neighborhood they live in or what school they attend.

Because the emotional ramifications of peer-to-peer harassment for victims are sometimes overshadowed by emphasis on prevention and punishment of aggressors, this chapter highlights the importance of victim support.

The overarching theme in bullying behaviors is that it involves one or more children causing physical and/or emotional harm to another child. When this harm becomes a pattern occurring over time, the cumulative effects can be even more damaging. Feelings of isolation, demoralization, insecurity, embarrassment, fear, anger, and sadness are common. Girls are sometimes targeted for sexual forms of harassment, which can be particularly harmful and humiliating. As with any hurtful or frightening experience in which a person has limited control, a bullied student may try to limit the harm through such behaviors as avoidance of certain peers or places, general social withdrawal, seeking help from adults, showing distress through crying or yelling, or even increased aggression. However, some students may appear less disrupted by the experience of being bullied. There is variation in individual reactions. Factors such as the severity and duration of the mistreatment and the existence of effective coping skills and social supports can also play an important role.

Without appropriate care and guidance, victims of bullying may suffer long term problems with negative self-opinions and fear of further harm. Some exhibit declines in academics, extracurricular activities, and functioning at home. Serious disturbances of mood and behavior can also be precipitated by such mistreatment by peers.

Recommendations

∼∼∼∼∼∼∼∼∼∼ CLASSROOM STRUCTURE ∼∼∼∼∼∼∼

Ask Yourself

When was the last time you had an opportunity to talk with your class about respectful behavior toward each other? (With older students, these topics sometimes surface less often.)

- *Do not let it slide:* Intimidation, insults, degradation, mockery, and other hurtful behaviors may escalate if adults do not address them. It is important to set an appropriate example. Of course, educators cannot intervene every time students have a minor conflict, and students need to learn to work some conflicts out on their own. However, the days of believing that bullying just makes victims tougher are gone.

- *Keep bystanders in mind:* Even children not directly involved as aggressors or recipients of bullying can be affected. Watching someone else get harassed can intimidate onlookers and be upsetting to many.

- *Hold aggressors responsible:* Be sure to place the consequences and restrictions where they belong. Exclusively telling the bullied student to simply stay away from the bullies or to avoid places in which bullying occurs takes away the victim's power and gives the bullying child a more dominant position. A better solution might be to restrict the aggressors from places or situations in which they target other children.

- *Make reports possible:* Foster an atmosphere in which students feel comfortable reporting concerns about bullying. Mention bullying from time to time, and encourage students to ask for support if they need it.

- *Set the tone:* Talk about bullying and other types of mistreatment early in the year, and regularly raise these topics. Let students know that this is something you take seriously and will directly address through both in-class interventions and referrals to administrators. Mentioning bullying prevention to the class does not have to take long, but it can have an important impact.

Keep in Mind

- Prevention can be just as important as intervention. Early identification of students who need support, and talking with your class about the importance of treating others with respect, can prevent problems from occurring both inside and outside the classroom.

~~~~~ COLLABORATING WITH STUDENTS ~~~~~

Ask Yourself

If you have noticed one student being targeted, might there be others who are not as likely to express concerns or to ask for support?

- *Respect autonomy:* When addressing a student who you think is being harassed, use language that does not inadvertently make the student feel powerless. Some students might ask you to help take responsibility for the problem, and that is okay. Others will feel demoralized by bullying and will benefit from empowerment. In such instances, let the student suggest what he hopes will change, and use "we" language, when possible, to help the student feel included in the solution. Of course, adults have to take on responsibility for many things, but validating the student's part in the solution, however small, can make a difference.

- *Praise courage:* Let a bullied student know that it takes courage to speak up and ask for help. Those are the first steps in addressing the problem. It really does take courage. Some children keep quiet about bullying for years because they feel ashamed about being victimized. Or, when they start to raise the topic with adults, they felt subtly invalidated, causing them to become quiet again.

- *Ask before advising:* When working with a large class, it is difficult to address every student issue and still have time to teach. Many problems can be quickly addressed throughout the day. However, if a student reports being bullied or you suspect that the student is being seriously mistreated, make sure you give space for the student to explain the problem. Also, ask a few questions to get a sense of the severity: "What insults have they said to you?" "Has he hurt you physically?" "What are you afraid she might do to you?" Sometimes, adults just observe the tip of the iceberg.

- *Suggest safety options:* If a child has ongoing concerns about being mistreated by peers, encourage him to use behaviors that may help reduce the impact: using assertive, nonaggressive statements to tell the peers to stop; walking away; telling an adult; spending free time with peers who are safe.

- *Leave it on the table:* Even if a child who may be bullied declines your support, let the child know that you and other staff will make yourselves available if he needs you in the future. You can help keep the topic alive by occasionally checking in with the student.

Keep in Mind

- If you have not attended formal training on how to identify and manage bullying in an educational setting, you should consider requesting such training from your school.

COLLABORATING WITH THE FAMILY/CAREGIVERS

Ask Yourself

How might family members feel if they know that their child is being emotionally or physically hurt?

- *Anticipate reactions:* Parents may understandably feel sad, frightened, angered, or defensive when they know their child is in pain. It can be emotionally upsetting for an education professional to field the family's reactions when a child has been mistreated. Be prepared for different responses from the caregivers: visible distress, anger toward the school and its professionals, or a sense of urgency to resolve the problems.

- *Get the full picture:* Ask the family to explain what they know about the situation and how the child has reacted at home. Sometimes, young people are able to contain distress in one setting (e.g., school) but appear much more upset in another setting (e.g., home). Collaborating with the family will help all parties gain a better sense of the situation and will help you decide whether a referral is necessary.

- *Collaborate to build on strengths:* Work with the caregivers to find activities that help increase the child's confidence and sense of accomplishment. This may help balance the demoralizing effects of being teased or harassed.

Keep in Mind

- When a child is being hurt, all adults involved in the child's care at school and at home may feel helpless or responsible. Because these situations evoke strong feelings, tensions can run high.

REFERRAL TO AN ADMINISTRATOR, COUNSELOR, OR MENTAL HEALTH PROFESSIONAL

Ask Yourself

How long has this student been harassed?

What changes have you noticed?

What concerns do you have about safety?

Consider such a step when

- You feel intimidated by an aggressive student, or you think that a student poses a danger to classmates, adults, or himself or herself. Remember: If you feel unsafe, access your supports right away.
- Interventions to support the bullied child or to stop the harassment have been unsuccessful, or you suspect that the student requires more assistance than he is currently receiving.
- You observe changes in a bullied student's mood, and you suspect that these changes are connected to mistreatment by peers.
- You see evidence of physical harm to a bullied child: red marks, bruises, torn clothing, etc.

Keep in Mind

- Consult early and often. When dealing with issues of bullying or abuse, talk to colleagues at school, and follow protocols that might require you to report your concerns to others.

WHAT TO EXPECT

In response to Jonathan's statement that it is "no big deal," you tell him that his safety and well-being are important to you and that the teachers and administrators of the school take any kind of harassment or bullying very seriously. You tell Jonathan that you know he is trying hard to keep up his high academic standards and that you admire his dedication. Finally, you acknowledge that it can be scary to ask for help, but you tell him that you have seen bad situations get much better when students were willing to talk about what was happening and work with school officials. Through this interaction, you have let Jonathan know that even if he does not want to talk about it now, you and the other adults at the school are always available to him, and there is hope for a solution. He is also now aware that others see his strengths and positive qualities, and you have communicated to him that seeking help may be seen as an act of courage rather than one of cowardice.

You continue to regularly check in with Jonathan to keep the lines of communication open, even though he often dismisses your efforts as unnecessary or even bothersome. After several weeks, however, Jonathan approaches you one day after school. You are quick to offer encouragement and reassurance that talking with you is safe and will likely lead to improvements. You are also careful to ask about the specifics of the situation to gather information needed to maintain his safety, and you seek his input for possible solutions so that he will see himself as an active participant in this process rather than a passive recipient of help. As the problem becomes clearer, some possible solutions emerge. You let Jonathan know that because this is so important, you want to include others who can also help. You consult with your school administrator and develop a plan that will involve coordination with Jonathan, his family, school administrators, and the school counselor. Your school has a detailed protocol in place to address bullying, but Jonathan's plan would not have been initiated without your observations, sensitivity, and persistence.

DISCUSSION QUESTIONS

1. What long-term effect can bullying have on how a young person thinks and feels about himself? How can educators' interventions help ameliorate those effects?

2. What is the line between less harmful teasing and bullying? How can you explain this difference to your students?

3. How might bullying differ among elementary, middle, and high school students? Do victims of bullying respond differently on the basis of age?

4. Why has bullying become such a prevalent topic in today's media and educational literature?

The following page is a handout for students who may have been bullied. You can also distribute it to the entire class because any student can benefit from this information, and we do not always know which students have been affected by bullying. This version is geared toward junior and senior high school students.

Bullying: What You Should
Know and What You Can Do About It

Bullying is deliberately causing harm to someone else through words or actions. It can include name calling, criticism, making fun of someone, excluding someone from activities, writing negative things online, or posting pictures of another person without his or her approval. Bullying can also include pushing, punching, spitting, or any other form of physically hurting someone or invading his or her personal space. Threatening to hurt or embarrass someone is also bullying.

Being bullied can make you feel scared, unsafe, embarrassed, ashamed, angry, demoralized, sad, or anxious.

If you have been bullied, you might

- Stop going places or stop talking to certain people to avoid situations in which you might be mistreated
- Experience changes in your sleeping, eating, mood, or attitude
- Act defensive or withdrawn, even around people who care about you
- Think there is nothing you can do to avoid being bullied again

What you can do if you have been bullied

- Do not just keep it to yourself! There are people who care and can help you. Talk privately with a family member, teacher, or trusted adult. Let your friends know how you are feeling.
- Keep your cool.
- Turn rude comments into a joke, or brush them off. Bullies often like to get a reaction and may stop if they do not.
- Spend your time around people who do not treat you this way. You do not deserve it.

What you can do if you see someone else get bullied

- Let the bullied peer know you think it is wrong that he or she was treated that way.
- Show your strength by never laughing or joining in hurting someone else.
- Change the subject to help get the attention off the peer being mistreated.
- Be inclusive: Ask a classmate who is being isolated to sit with you.
- Let adults know what is going on so that they can help.

Remember: Bullying can hurt a lot. But it does not have to be your problem alone. Talk to people you trust if you are being mistreated at school or elsewhere.

Recognize and Respond to Emotional and Behavioral Issues in the Classroom: A Teacher's Guide by Andrew Jonathan Cole, Psy.D.,
& Aaron M. Shupp, Psy.D. Copyright © 2012 by Paul H. Brookes Publishing Co. All rights reserved.

Chapter 10

Personal Boundaries

As a new student, Naomi seemed to fit right in to your second-grade classroom. She did not need much time to warm up to you or the other students. After a few days, it seemed like she had been in the classroom since the beginning of the year. Her outgoing nature made a positive impression on the other students and the adults she came into contact with. Although you work hard to make your students feel comfortable in the classroom, Naomi's level of comfort and familiarity left you feeling uneasy.

It soon became apparent that even though Naomi did not seem to have any problems adjusting to her new surroundings, she might need help in other ways. You first became concerned when you noticed how Naomi befriended peers and adults as if they were close, longtime friends. She would often hug people that she had just met, and it was not unusual for her to share private details of her home life with new acquaintances. These disclosures, along with the personal questions she asked of others, often led to awkward interactions.

Naomi was constantly lending her personal belongings to other students and even giving away items. Students soon began asking her for things because she seemed so eager to lend or give away her belongings, and she certainly would not say "no" to a request. When you observed her offering another student a personal item that you were certain her guardians would not want her to give away, you stepped in to intervene. Naomi reacted with surprise and shock. She insisted that the other student was her friend and that she wanted to help her. For the first time, you saw a flash of anger in Naomi's eyes, and she accused you of hating her.

WHAT YOU MIGHT SEE

- Difficulty saying "no" to others
- Excessive lending or giving away of personal items
- Overly affectionate—hugging, touching, staying in close proximity
- Indiscriminately sharing personal information
- Excessive need to please or be accepted by others
- Frequently giving gifts, or giving gifts with unusually high value
- Overly trusting new people, or overestimating the level of closeness with new acquaintances
- Asking personal questions or frequently seeking personal information about others
- Difficulty understanding why others do not readily share personal information
- Feeling rejected if others attempt to set limits or establish boundaries in the relationship

DESCRIPTION OF PROBLEMS

The term *boundaries* describes the level of physical and emotional closeness that a person is comfortable with in a social interaction. Each individual sets her own boundaries, often without being consciously aware of doing so. These boundaries help individuals maintain a sense of safety, comfort, and control in their relations with others. In a social interaction, a person generally gives cues defining the boundaries of the relationship and picks up on the cues of others. This unspoken communication provides a framework that helps people know what is and is not acceptable in a particular interaction. Boundaries vary based on the type of relationship, duration of the relationship, environmental context, culture, and other factors.

Although some people might not respect (or might even violate) the boundaries of others, this chapter is focused on individuals who have difficulty setting or maintaining appropriate boundaries for themselves. Learning how to set boundaries with others is a typical part of child and adolescent development. However, some children may experience more severe problems in this area. A child's past experiences might have taught her that personal boundaries will not be respected and that efforts to set boundaries are, therefore, not worthwhile. Boundary difficulties may be driven by a desire to stay connected with others because of fears of being abandoned or rejected. In some cases, the child may have simply not learned how to distinguish varying levels of intimacy in relationships. Low self-worth, insecurity, or a need for control over the environment may sometimes be related to boundary problems.

Problems with boundaries can contribute to ongoing relationship difficulties. If a child does not learn how to establish healthy boundaries, social relationships are likely to be volatile and short-lived. Problems such as depressed moods and anxiety can result. In some cases, difficulty setting boundaries can lead to an increased risk of being mistreated or victimized.

Recommendations

CLASSROOM STRUCTURE

Ask Yourself

What personal boundaries are needed for a student to be successful in my classroom?

- *Self-monitor:* Be aware of your own boundaries. Often, your first indication that something is different or unusual with regard to boundaries will be a visceral reaction rather than a conscious observation. Trust your instincts. Ask yourself, "Is this something I would do or say with any student?"

- *Observe:* Is the student having difficulty with boundaries with just one person or several people, or is the problem more generalized? Is the problem in a specific class or at a particular time? Your observations will help you understand the extent of the problem and may even point to a different problem (e.g., bullying, peer rejection, peer pressure).

- *Impose boundaries:* Consider rules regarding sharing or giving of items, personal touch, or seating arrangements, as appropriate for your classroom.

- Remain watchful: Some problems with boundaries may cause obvious disruptions in your classroom. However, some problems will not be obvious at all. Keep an eye out for students who do not present obvious behavioral problems. What are their relationships like? Are they well liked for positive reasons, or are they being taken advantage of?

- *Related problems:* Be alert for signs that other problems may be present. Does the student appear down? Do you see signs of low self-esteem or poor self-worth? These problems likely need to be brought to the attention of the school counselor or a mental health professional.

Keep in Mind

- You are likely to feel something is not quite right with a student who has problems with personal boundaries before you can put your finger on the exact problem.

~~~~~~~~~~~~~~~ ## COLLABORATING WITH STUDENTS ~~~~~~~~~~~~~~~

Ask Yourself

What specific behaviors are causing problems for this student?

What would need to be different for this student to not have problems with boundaries?

- *Lead by example:* Remember that sometimes your example is more powerful that what you say. When you keep appropriate boundaries with a student who is struggling in this regard, you are demonstrating that you can set comfortable limits for yourself without rejecting or disliking the other person.

- *Prepare:* Try to anticipate personal questions that a student may ask, and prepare answers ahead of time. This will help you not feel awkward or defensive when asked. Of course, you cannot prepare for every question that a student with poor boundaries may ask, but this will help you come up with strategies for maintaining your personal boundaries when these situations arise.

- *Check in:* Ask the student about your observations to better understand her perspective (e.g., "Julia, I noticed earlier that you let someone borrow your ruler, but you needed your ruler for the project you were working on. Help me understand why you let someone borrow it when you needed it").

- *Clear expectations:* By setting clear expectations, you are modeling assertiveness, even as you are helping the student learn appropriate boundaries (e.g., "When you are working on the project that involves the ruler, I expect you to keep your ruler so that you can complete the project").

- *Give examples:* Remember that a student who has difficulty setting boundaries may not know how to do so appropriately. For example, it might help a student understand how to set boundaries with a peer if you were to say, "Naomi, if I were in your shoes, I might say something like, 'Julia, I'd be happy to let you borrow my ruler another time, but right now I need it to complete the assignment, so I can't let you borrow it.'"

- *Emphasize the positive:* Point out the student's positive characteristics (e.g., "You are obviously a very kind friend"). Doing so will show the student that you are helping her learn more effective ways to demonstrate her positive qualities. A student with poor boundaries likely believes that the way she has been doing things is the best or only way, and the student may need this type of encouragement to keep an open mind.

- *Normalize:* Remind the student that part of being a good friend and growing up is learning how to stand up for oneself and set limits with others, as well as learning how different types of relationships have different boundaries.

Keep in Mind

- Be prepared for your boundaries to be challenged, and remember that, by setting healthy parameters, you are modeling a critical aspect of social interactions.

~~~~~~~~~ COLLABORATING WITH THE FAMILY/CAREGIVERS ~~~~~~~~~

Ask Yourself

How can I describe the problem in a way that is clear, nonjudgmental, and based on direct observations?

- *Share observations:* Remember to stay focused on the specific behavior you have observed and the problems it is causing in your classroom. Avoid using labels or diagnostic terms, and do not assume causes.

- *Find similar concerns:* After sharing what you have seen, ask whether the family has noticed any similar problems in other areas. This may be difficult with boundary problems because they are not as easy to define and may be hidden by more prominent symptoms, or they may be accepted as typical behavior for the child. Some prompting may be necessary (e.g., "Have others ever commented on similar problems? What do you see as the child's strengths and weaknesses? What feedback have you received from other teachers about the student?").

- *Prepare:* These are difficult problems to identify and address. Be prepared that you may be the first person to bring up the problems with the family. Have specific examples in mind. If you are questioned as to why you are the first to bring this up, reiterate that you can only share your observations and that your concern is helping the student be as successful as possible in your classroom.

- *Maintain your boundaries:* Just as you model appropriate boundaries for the student, you should be prepared to maintain boundaries with the family. Decide ahead of time what questions you are comfortable answering about yourself and your experience, and plan how you will respond to questions that you are not comfortable answering.

Keep in Mind

- Developing a positive relationship with the family is key. Successfully changing a problem with boundaries will likely require the family's involvement.

~~~~~~~~ REFERRAL TO AN ADMINISTRATOR, ~~~~~~~~
COUNSELOR, OR MENTAL HEALTH PROFESSIONAL

Ask Yourself

Have I seen similar problems before? If so, how have I addressed them, and what were the outcomes?

Consider such a step when

- You see or suspect that physical boundaries are being violated for any student.

- A student appears uncomfortable and unable to manage problems related to personal boundaries.

- Your attempts to help the student set limits in relationships are met with emotional distress, outbursts, or even greater behavioral problems.

- Your interactions with the family suggest that family involvement may be necessary to really address the student's difficulties.

Keep in Mind

- The cause of boundary problems may be complex and multifaceted. Do not feel like you should be expected to address these problems on your own. Use your support system!

WHAT TO EXPECT

Even if it is hard to define, Naomi's problem is becoming more apparent. Carefully documenting some of your observations has helped provide clarity and direction. In the past few days, you have seen Naomi give away personal items, run out of line to hug a school administrator, ask a staff member for her home address, and give away most of her lunch because another student asked for it.

You plan to individually address Naomi and then use this opportunity to teach about boundaries in an age-appropriate way to your class. One of your classroom expectations is for all students to treat each other with respect. Revisiting this with the entire class provides a natural opportunity to discuss personal space and the need to ask permission before hugging or touching someone else, without singling out Naomi.

When you individually meet with Naomi, you emphasize her caring and outgoing nature and stress that part of growing up is learning how to respect the personal space of others and stand up for oneself when needed. You give Naomi examples of different relationships and explain when a hug might be appropriate or when a handshake, high five, or fist bump might be more appropriate. You also suggest that when she feels like giving a friend a gift, she could try telling the friend something she likes about her. Showing that you understand how important it is for her to be a good friend seems to help make Naomi open to these suggestions.

In preparation for contacting Naomi's family, you identify some of the specific observations you want to share to illustrate the problems that need to be addressed. You also write down some specific questions that might help you understand the family's perspective. Being aware that you may need to assert your own boundaries, you consider how you will respond to questions that are not related to Naomi's problems, and how you will redirect the conversation back to the topic if faced with personal questions.

DISCUSSION QUESTIONS

1. Recall a time when you felt that your boundaries were being pushed. What happened? How did you handle it? How did you prepare for similar situations that might arise in the future?

2. How have problems with personal boundaries affected your teaching? Can you think of a student who had difficulty setting limits in relationships? How did this affect you, the student's peers, and/or other teachers?

3. What problems might arise in the future for a student who has difficulty setting personal boundaries?

> *You can modify the following handout to suit the age or specific needs of your students. It is best if this worksheet is completed with the assistance of an adult. This example is written for elementary or middle school students.*

WHAT YOU MIGHT SEE

- Misreading social cues (continuing to talk when peers are trying to move on to a new subject or activity)
- Limited expression of emotion or a quick shift between a neutral expression and agitation
- Overemphasis on unique interests or hobbies to which same-age peers have trouble relating
- Seemingly immature or notably precocious ways of viewing the world (e.g., a teenager who prefers to talk about cartoons meant for younger children; a fourth grader who points out complexities about school subjects that his or her peers are unable to recognize)
- Emotional outbursts of sadness, irritation, or disappointment that seem inappropriate to the situation
- Asserting that there is only one answer to a discussion question or only one way to perform a task
- Excessively correcting other students' behavior
- Being overly compliant or underassertive with peers

DESCRIPTION OF THE PROBLEMS

There are other social, emotional, and communication problems that affect children's behavior in academic settings but are not addressed elsewhere in this book. Some of these difficulties include frequent, non-aggressive emotional dysregulation, such as crying or yelling when frustrated; communication impairments, such as isolating oneself when distressed rather than asking for help, or having difficulty putting words to what one wants to express; and social problems, including less developed interpersonal skills or trouble reading social cues. All of these issues can affect a child's ability to learn or can lead to other difficulties in the classroom.

For some children, these problems are influenced by biological predispositions that cause them to express emotion, interpret interactions, or absorb information from the environment in ways that differ from the majority of their peers. Other children have not had the right guidance regarding how to better manage feelings and relationships or to communicate their needs. Because of limits on resources and time, educational systems use standard learning techniques that work for most children. However, students whose needs differ significantly from the majority often struggle to keep up, to sustain attention, or to conform to behavioral expectations.

Some students with diagnosed learning disabilities, auditory or cognitive processing disorders, or characteristics on the autism spectrum may receive special assistance or accommodations. If you are working with a student who you know has a diagnosed problem, you should consult resources that provide specialized background information and recommendations for how to support youths with the respective diagnosis.

However, not all children with nonstandard learning needs qualify for individualized education program or meet criteria for diagnoses of educational or mental health problems. Consequently, skilled educators who provide effective structure and communication with each student play important roles in these students' educational adjustment. Without the support of skilled educators, family members, and health care professionals, such students may fall through the cracks of traditional education systems and, thus, not reach their full academic potential. It is important to remember that success in educational settings is not necessarily representative of performance in other areas of life. A number of students who never excel in academia flourish when they enter work environments that suit their skills, interests, and styles for relating to the world. The encouragement they receive in school can translate to success in life, even if they persistently struggle in school.

Recommendations

~~~~~~~~~~ CLASSROOM STRUCTURE ~~~~~~~~~~

Ask Yourself

In what ways do the classroom expectations already encourage this child's educational development?

What classroom expectations does this student struggle to meet?

- *Lay foundations for positive interaction:* If a student is frequently rejected or isolated, be sensitive to situations that may feel awkward for her. Sometimes, assigning students to work groups or encouraging students who tend to isolate themselves to join with students who are tolerant and accepting will facilitate positive social interactions.

- *Recognize individual differences:* Remember that one size does not fit all. For example, some students may benefit from downtime during the day to decompress, whereas others benefit from constant interaction. If a student appears to hang back during free time to read, draw, or independently play, this is not always a bad thing. Some children need alone time to rejuvenate themselves. If you do have a concern, consider the full picture (e.g., Does the child appear happy when independently playing, or does she appear to feel rejected by peers? Does she play alone occasionally or all the time? What does the child prefer to do if all options are available to her?).

- *Offer examples:* Provide concrete examples of how the student could change his or her behavior. If a student who tends to think in fixed, inflexible ways attempts to debate others in an overly persistent, verbose manner, give specific alternatives for how she could otherwise approach the situation. You might say, "Beth, it's good that you share your opinions. We also need to listen to other people's opinions. After you make one point, then you need to pause to let others share what they think." Or, you could say, "Beth, try speaking for only 30 seconds, and when that time is up, stop speaking and give others a chance to respond."

- *Encourage meaningful goals:* Consider small steps that might help the student adapt to the classroom setting. Discuss those goals with the student, and provide rationale for why the goals are important and how they will benefit the student.

Keep in Mind

- Behaviors and adaptive skills that seem easy to grasp for most students might not seem obvious to others. Explaining the purpose and specific steps involved in reaching those goals can help enlist the student's cooperation.

COLLABORATING WITH STUDENTS

Ask Yourself

Is there anything unique about what motivates this child?

Does the student appear to have difficulty sustaining motivation in class?

- *Acknowledge, then set limits:* Offer a balance between recognition of feelings and age-appropriate boundaries for students who are prone to outbursts of emotion. Such outbursts can include excessive yelling, tearfulness, or tantrums related to sadness, disappointment, or frustration and can be disruptive both to the student's learning and to the class as a whole. For instance, if a child loses an educational game during class and begins to loudly and tearfully complain, feel free to acknowledge his or her disappointment: "It looks like you feel very disappointed and sad about not winning. I'm sorry you feel that way." Then, redirect the student toward managing his or her feelings in a way that is appropriate for the classroom: "We need to continue with class now. Is there something you can do to help yourself feel more calm and focus on the next lesson?"

- *Encourage!* When a student who has difficulty navigating social and emotional challenges appears to struggle with motivation to continue trying to learn new skills, try the following strategies.

  - Remind the child of small steps of growth she has already made, and praise those steps.

- Help the child consider his or her reasons for trying in the first place, whether it is to get along better with peers, feel good about his or her accomplishments in school, receive fewer consequences for disruptive behaviors, or gain a reward for his or her efforts.

- Normalize the struggle. Who does not have areas in need of personal growth? Although each student (and every adult) has to strive to make positive changes throughout life, she also has to weigh the good with the bad and accept who she is in the present. Students who suffer a lot of frustration and disappointment in school sometimes need to be reminded of this.

- *Appeal to individual interests:* Some students have specific subjects or hobbies that fascinate them or provide a lot of pleasure. If you get to know a little about the child's interests, you can use them as incentives for appropriate behavior. For instance, Jameel may not respond to the typical rewards and consequences used in class. However, he loves to talk about airplanes and is constantly drawing them. You could allow him to involve airplanes in his next project if he does not disrupt class by speaking out of turn during the next week.

- *Ask for feedback:* Elicit the student's opinions about what helps her achieve in the classroom. The insightful answers children sometimes provide can be surprising.

Keep in Mind

- Even if you are not sure about the underlying reasons for a student's difficulties, providing encouragement, incentives, and structure may still prove beneficial.

COLLABORATING WITH THE FAMILY/CAREGIVERS

Ask Yourself

How might communication with the caregivers advance your efforts to reduce the student's disruptions in class or to help the student increase adaptive behaviors? What behaviors do you reinforce in the classroom that the parents might also be able to encourage from their child?

- *Anticipate miscommunications:* Some students with these difficulties also have trouble communicating social and academic problems to their families. Parents may ask their children questions about school but receive limited information or explanations based on unique interpretations of events. If a child has trouble providing information to his or her parents, it is not unusual for parents to call with concerns or questions that may indicate misunderstandings.

- *Keep the dialogue alive:* Let the family share their ideas about what type of encouragement or limits they feel the child requires to succeed. If you are able to integrate suggestions from the parents into your work with the child, let the parents know that their suggestions proved helpful.

- *Make first contact:* If parents have not contacted you, consider initiating communication related to the following concerns.

  - How the student's social, emotional, or communication problems are affecting his or her learning goals

  - The types of situations that the student struggles to manage during class. If a parent is made more aware of the problem, he or she may be better prepared to intervene.

  - How communication between you and the caregivers might improve the student's motivation or skills for functioning in class

Keep in Mind

- When parents sound anxious about their child's well-being in school or ask pointed questions about how you are planning to help their child, try not to take it personally. It can be extremely stressful for the whole family when a child struggles in school.

REFERRAL TO AN ADMINISTRATOR, COUNSELOR, OR MENTAL HEALTH PROFESSIONAL

Ask Yourself

Are the student's difficulties causing her significant distress?

Do you feel that the child's inability to adjust to the classroom setting is caused by more than a minor skill deficit?

Consider such a step when

- You notice unusual habits or patterns in the student's attempts to complete academic tasks, in addition to some of the problems described above. Children sometimes develop their own ways to cope with undiagnosed sensory, learning, communication, or emotional challenges.

- You have other reason to suspect that the child could have an underlying issue that might require evaluation from another education or health care professional.

- The child might benefit from additional programming offered by your school. Many schools now offer groups for teaching social skills, emotion management, study habits, or other adaptive skills.

- The student does not respond to typical classroom interventions and may require a creative approach.

Keep in Mind

- Many emotional, communication, or social problems can be difficult to clearly identify without the involvement of specialized education or health care professionals. Sometimes, a quick consultation with another professional who conducts evaluations can help put the student's behaviors into context.

WHAT TO EXPECT

Because Meg's difficulties are not easily understood, you decide to focus on what you observe in class. Two issues stand out as areas to target for improvement: her repeated questions and statements that slow down lessons and irritate other students; and her habit of leaving the classroom when other students express frustration or irritation about her behavior.

Meg's repeated questions and statements indicate a strong interest in the material being presented. You understand that this keeps her motivated, and you want to encourage her interest. However, you also need to keep moving to cover all of the material and to keep other students engaged. You formulate concrete guidelines for Meg to follow. You encourage her to ask questions or make comments when she wants to; you emphasize that her interest is very positive and that you want her to continue contributing to group discussions. However, you also let her know that she must learn to limit her questions or comments so that you will have time to cover all the material and others will have the chance to participate. You propose that, after she asks a question or makes a comment, she wait until three other students have asked questions or made comments before she does so again. After presenting you with some "what if" scenarios to improve her understanding, Meg seems comfortable with the concrete nature of this arrangement, and you emphasize that letting others participate in a discussion is an important skill that everyone must learn.

Your second goal for Meg is for her to stay in class even when faced with strong emotions, such as being harshly spoken to by other students. Again, you focus on normalizing the need to get away from stressful situations and take a break. As you ask Meg for her ideas, she tells you that, when she leaves the classroom, she goes to a certain part of the hallway where student awards are displayed, and she reads about the awards even if she has done so before. She indicates that she likes to do this, and she mentions other things she likes to read. Meg agrees to bring in a folder with papers to read on topics of interest; when she needs a break, she will go to a designated area of the room for 5 minutes to look at her folder. This is not your ultimate goal for Meg—you would prefer that she stay focused on the lesson throughout the class period—but it seems like a good place to start.

DISCUSSION QUESTIONS

1. Do social, emotional, and communication problems exist on spec-
    trums (i.e., we all have some impairments and strengths), or are
    these problems finite?

2. What is a reasonable amount of time and effort to devote to a stu-
    dent who is struggling with such problems? How do you know
    when you are doing all that you can and that you are reaching your
    own limits?

3. If you were a student who was accustomed to feeling frustrated
    and disappointed in school, what might you like to hear from
    educators?

4. What are some unique or individualized approaches you have used
    to help students in the past?

---

*Knowing when and where to express certain emotions can be confus-
ing to many children. Helping a student understand what is expected
of her often requires more than the redirections that adults provide
after inappropriate outbursts. This is particularly true for students
who have had less guidance about these subjects at home or who
have innate difficulty recognizing social expectations. The following
form is a simple and brief outline you can use to collaboratively set
expectations for emotional expression in situations that have already
proven problematic. Sometimes, a written record can assist a student
in seeing what is being asked of her. Remember that this may not be
sufficient to alter the student's behavior, but it is one more tool to
support positive change.*

Trying New Ways of Dealing with Feelings

Something in school that is difficult to deal with:

How this makes me feel:

What I do when I feel this way in school:

How others respond when I do this:

Something different I can do to deal with this next time:

In the next week, I will _____ (new behavior) instead of _____ (current behavior) when I feel _____.

_____

To be filled out in 1 week

The situations in which I tried the new behavior:

How I felt after the new behavior:

How others responded:

Chapter 12

Engaging the Family

At the beginning of the school year, you make a point to contact the guardians of each of your students. You have found that establishing relationships with them early in the year sets a positive tone and pays off when you have to notify them of behavioral problems or enlist their help with particular concerns.

When you first call Jeremiah's mother, she does not seem interested in talking with you. She gives no response to your introduction and provides only curt responses to your questions. As you search for a way to connect with her, she begins questioning you about your teaching experience. She asks how long you have been teaching and where you have taught. She asks whether you know Mr. Greene at a school across town; she says he was excellent with Jeremiah and is probably the only teacher Jeremiah has ever respected. She questions your education and asks whether you have heard of a certain author. She responds with surprise when you say that you have not. As you find yourself unnerved and wanting to end the call, she asks whether you have children. You quickly consider how to answer that question, realizing that her line of questioning has become intrusive and may be intended to undermine your credibility.

During the next several weeks, you notice that Jeremiah seems to be pushing limits in your classroom more than he previously had. Of course, you would rather not call his home, but it seems necessary given his change in behavior. Jeremiah seems aware that you and his mother are not on the same page, and you believe he is taking advantage of this.

WHAT YOU MIGHT SEE

- Guardians who seem uninterested in what you say, dismiss your feedback, blame you for the student's difficulties, or avoid working toward positive changes
- Families who may need additional help understanding the problem or education regarding the effects of the problematic behaviors
- Family members who challenge you, respond to you with hostility, or engage in acts of intimidation
- Families who support, excuse, or enable the problematic behavior
- Families who expect criticism and blame and, therefore, start their interactions with you from a position of guardedness and suspicion
- Caregivers who themselves had negative experiences in school and, therefore, do not trust the school system, you as the teacher, or other educators to have the child's best interest at heart
- Families who are stricken by hardships, whether from physical or mental illness, social factors, emotional turmoil, or financial stressors. These family members may be too overwhelmed to believe that they can contribute or work with you.

DESCRIPTION OF PROBLEMS

This chapter is designed to provide general guidance for working with families. Although some common problem areas are mentioned above to illustrate the range of difficulties that can arise, the focus is on general principles that can improve collaboration with guardians rather than on addressing specific problems. The term *family* is broadly defined to encompass all guardians and caregivers that might be involved in the child's life.

As a teacher, you have experience with a wide range of families. Some are immediately and consistently supportive, some are more challenging, and some are so overwhelmed with their own struggles that they feel unable to be anything more than minimally involved.

Of course, some families *do* contribute to the problems you see in your classroom. However, this should not be your focus. Most families want the best for their children. The difference between a supportive guardian and one who is challenging to work with is often a simple matter of differences in knowledge, skills, emotional factors, and environmental challenges.

Recommendations

Ask Yourself

What is the goal for this student?

What would be helpful from the family to achieve this goal?

- *Starting point:* Remember, the vast majority of guardians want the best for their children. Always start with this assumption.

- *Share positives:* Most guardians like to hear positive things about their children. Even when you are addressing problem behaviors, a balanced report is more likely to be well received. Before you talk to the guardian, think about the student's strengths and what you personally like about the student.

- *Prepare:* Think of what you want to say before you call. What are the main points you want to make? Try to limit your focus to a maximum of two or three points.

- *Collaborate:* If you are asking the family to help with a student problem, be prepared to offer something that you are willing to do to help. How can you demonstrate your investment in improving the problem?

- *Offer resources:* If you think it might be necessary, prepare contact information for individuals who may be able to offer additional assistance, such as school counselors or administrators, or provide a list of community resources. You can even offer to assist with linkage to these services, such as introducing a family member to the school counselor and being involved in these services.

- *Maintain contact:* Stay in regular communication with family members as much as possible, even when the student is not having any difficulty. The relationships you establish early on, and in times of student success, will be enormously helpful when you have to work on difficulties.

- *Narrow scope:* Stay focused on how the problematic behavior is affecting the student in your class. Avoid speculating too widely about causes or straying too far from what you observe. This approach will make it clear that your concern is the student's success in the classroom, and it will help you stay focused in the event that the guardian attempts to change the focus (or puts the focus on you).

- *Avoid labels:* If you think about a family in generalizations (e.g., difficult, uncooperative), you will likely underestimate the strengths that family members have to offer or the progress that they can make. Look for the positives, just as you would with a student. If you see no possibility of engaging the family or working collaboratively toward an improved outcome for the student, the family will likely perceive this, and a positive outcome is less likely.

Keep in Mind

- Find common ground, express your interest and commitment to the child, and avoid blaming. If you present yourself as a collaborator and resource for the family, your efforts are more likely to be well received.

REFERRAL TO AN ADMINISTRATOR, COUNSELOR, OR MENTAL HEALTH PROFESSIONAL

Consider such a step when

- The family members seem to have basic needs that interfere with their ability to fully support the student's education. Examples might include lack of adequate housing, food, medical care, or safety.

- The family appears to lack the basic skills necessary to support the student (e.g., parenting skills, conflict resolution) and may benefit from additional therapeutic intervention. Remember that counselors and mental health professionals are often trained to address these issues.

- Your efforts to establish a trusting relationship with the family are consistently ineffective. The family might view the larger school system with suspicion or distrust and would benefit from seeing the entire system in a more positive way. Consider team meetings (including administrators and/or school counselors) with the family to demonstrate the commitment of everyone involved to the success of the student.

- You suspect any form of abuse or maltreatment. Remember, you do not need to have any concrete evidence to share your concerns with your support team. If you have reason to suspect abuse or mistreatment, follow all state and local reporting procedures.

Keep in Mind

- Your concerns or difficulties with a family may reflect larger issues or needs. Stay focused on supporting the student in your classroom, and use your support team when needed.

WHAT TO EXPECT

For now, Jeremiah's behavioral problems are manageable, so before calling home to address his difficulties in your class, you make it a point to call several times over the next few weeks to share positive observations of Jeremiah. Your calls serve two purposes: You are building a relationship with Jeremiah's mother by making it clear that you are invested in his success, and you are monitoring what effect, if any, this contact has on Jeremiah. His mother is not overly friendly or receptive to any of your calls, but you remember that unless you establish a working relationship with her, it will be an uphill battle to make progress with Jeremiah.

To be genuine in your efforts at reaching out, you take a few minutes before each call to think of Jeremiah's positive qualities and interests, in addition to the observation that you want to share. And, although you do not know much about Jeremiah's mother, you take a few minutes to remember some of the things you do know about this family; this step provides a compassionate perspective and helps you avoid taking any negative reactions personally.

Another aspect of your preparation involves considering how you will respond to personal questions or any statements or questions designed to undermine your credibility. You remember to not react to any statements that are undermining and, instead, stay focused on the reason for your call. You also decide to freely answer any questions about your training or experience but to redirect personal questions. To do so, you think of ways to kindly decline to answer, such as, "Over the years, I've found my personal experiences are not the best thing to rely on. As you know, each family has a different approach, and in this case, you're the expert on Jeremiah. Usually, we get the best results when we combine my experience as a teacher and your expertise as the parent."

When it is time to address a problem with Jeremiah, you focus on one or two specific behaviors that you have recently observed. You avoid any labels or interpretations of the behavior and, instead, look to his mother as a collaborator. You ask whether she has ever seen anything similar. If she offers input, you thank her for her help and praise any efforts she has already made to address this problem. She volunteers her understanding of the behavior, which you take note of, along with any labels or descriptions she uses, so that you can use these same terms and descriptions in future conversations.

Although your interactions with Jeremiah's mother remain challenging, you are optimistic that some positive changes are occurring in your relationship that will lead to improved collaboration in the future. You know that maintaining a steady, calm, nonreactive demeanor is likely to lead to an improved working relationship over time.

DISCUSSION QUESTIONS

1. What are some types of challenges you have faced when working with families?

2. What was the most difficult family interaction you have had? What strategies did you use to get through it?

3. Have you ever felt that you just could not get through to a family /
    guardian? Looking back, what may have been the reasons for the
    difficulty, and what else could you or others have done to address
    these issues?

---

*The following form is a quick reference sheet for an education profes-
sional on the go who has only a short time to prepare before calling
or meeting with a guardian. This list is designed to reinforce recommendations above and to help you focus and prepare your approach
before speaking with a family. You can fill it out or just glance at it
for reference.*

Pre-contact Reference Sheet

Primary issue I need to address:

How this issue affects the student's learning or functioning in school:

Two strengths the student shows in class:

Two difficulties the student is having that relate to this issue:

What I am doing to help the student:

What the student needs to do to improve on this issue:

Two strengths the caregivers demonstrate in supporting their child:

The type of collaboration I would like to develop with the caregivers:

How things have changed since the last contact with caregivers:

References and Recommended Reading

Akin-Little, A., Little, S.G., Bray, M.A., & Kehle, T.J. (1999). *Behavioral interventions in schools: Evidence-based positive strategies.* Washington, DC: American Psychological Association.

Barkley, R.A. (2000). *Taking charge of ADHD: The complete authoritative guide for parents* (Rev. ed.). New York, NY: Guilford Press.

Barkley, R.A., & Benton, C.M. (1998). *Your defiant child: Eight steps to better behavior.* New York, NY: Guilford Press.

Barkley, R.A., & Robin, A.L. (2008). *Your defiant teen: Ten steps to resolve conflict and rebuild your relationships.* New York, NY: Guilford Press.

Corman, C.A., & Hallowell, E.M. (2005). *Positively ADD: Real success stories to inspire your dreams.* New York, NY: Walker Childrens.

Craig, S.E. (2008). *Reaching and teaching children who hurt: Strategies for your classroom.* Baltimore, MD: Paul H. Brookes Publishing Co.

Gonzalez-Mena, J. (2009). *50 strategies for communicating and working with diverse families* (2nd ed.). Upper Saddle River, NJ: Prentice Hall.

Hallowell, E.M., & Ratey, J.J. (2011). *Driven to distraction* (2nd ed.). New York, NY: Anchor.

Kearney, C. (2008). *Helping school refusing children and their parents: A guide for school-based professionals.* New York, NY: Oxford University Press.

Knoster, T.P. (2008). *The teacher's pocket guide for effective classroom management.* Baltimore, MD: Paul H. Brookes Publishing Co.

Medoff, L. (2010). *Resilience in the classroom: Helping students with special needs.* New York, NY: Kaplan.

Olsen, G.W., & Fuller, M.L. (2011). *Home and school relations: Teachers and parents working together* (4th ed.). Upper Saddle River, NJ: Prentice Hall.

Orpinas, P., & Horne, A.M. (2005). *Bullying prevention: Creating a positive school climate and developing social competence.* Washington, DC: American Psychological Association.

Seligman, M.E.P. (2007). *The optimistic child: A proven program to safeguard children against depression and build lifelong resilience.* New York, NY: Houghton Mifflin Harcourt.

Sprick, R.S. (2008). *Discipline in the secondary classroom: A positive approach to behavior management* (2nd ed.). San Francisco, CA: Jossey-Bass.

Wachtel, E.F. (1994). *Treating troubled children and their families.* New York, NY: Guilford Press.

ONLINE RESOURCES

American Psychological Association
Retrieved from www.apa.org

The Melissa Institute for Violence Prevention and Treatment
Retrieved from www.melissainstitute.org

NYU Child Study Center
Retrieved from www.AboutOurKids.org

It Gets Better
Retrieved from www.itgetsbetter.org

Index

Forms are indicated by *f.*